"By far the most thorough and well-structured guide to digital tr.   , ...
across. It's an invaluable resource to businesses at all stages of the process, providing insight
into digitalization and working with data in a clear and engaging way."

—Jiri Kobelka, CEO, Tatum

"This book explains, in simple language and with an abundance of examples, what digital
transformation is all about. The reader is taken through a journey supported by a rock-
solid technology and business content, while also learning about the risks and benefits.
A must read."

—Gabriele Rossi, Enterprise Architect, ABN Amro Bank

"This book is like a good architecture: It explains a really complex subject like Digital
Transformation in plain English! It does this by discussing the constituent parts and how
these parts interact and strengthen each other. All this is supported by beautiful, easy to
understand graphics. This book helps a lot in navigating where you stand as a company in
your Digital Transformation. Thomas and Roger, job well done!"

—Brian Lokhorst, Lead Architect SOA Competence Center,
Dutch Tax and Customs Organisation

"This is the book that needs to be read by anyone that wants to understand where contemporary
business and technology are going."

—Eric Barceló Monroy, Head of Technology Architecture Consulting,
Entra a la Gran Nube, SA de CV

"In this book the authors pulled off a small miracle—to demystify 'digital transformation' and
make it tangible and understandable—as it's so much more than technology, it's about people,
culture, data and putting customers into the center of the game."

—Clemens Utschig, CTO Boehringer Ingelheim

"Organizations struggle implementing digital transformation initiatives successfully. A Field
Guide to Digital Transformation *is a perfect recipe and a reference model to guide teams on*
concepts, technologies and solutions to deliver digital transformation efforts in a standard and
more effective way."

—Ramesh Aki, Staff VP – Digital Platforms and Engineering, Anthem, Inc.

"For any firm, achieving true digital transformation to become a differentiator in its industry is quite difficult. This new book on digital transformation is an excellent overview and first step towards this journey. It gives an executive level overview of the essential technologies, the processes one should follow to start that journey. This book also advises on how a firm must rethink its existing business models, deal with the changes, and retrain its employees for new skills with nice illustrations."

—Thirumurthi Ranganathan, MBA (a lifelong learner and senior architect with 20+ years of IT Architecture experience with 12 years in FinTech)

"A should-read book on managing technology business change for managers, executives, and strategists. I strongly recommend this book to anyone interested in the theory and practice of business change and transforming business using emerging technologies. The book provides a holistic and concise description of digital transformation; what it is, what is consists of in terms of terminology and technology, and how to use data and decision insight to drive transformation in action. The book uses well defined concepts to help the reader to capture what digital transformation is all about; from the early motivation and definition, to how it is done in action with examples.

With this book you will find easy-to-understand symbols and icons that illustrates for the reader the key concepts. The book is well structured in two parts; first the foundation part, and then next a practice part that puts attention to data and decision management in online solutions, shifting the mindset from product-centricity to customer-centricity. The authors show the importance of connecting business with processes, technology and data to construct the future operations. Through clear, engaging explanations to help the reader to establish the new processes."

—Morten R Stender, PhD, Partner of Staun&Stender

"Valuable insights in the organizational impact of disruptive technologies"

—Ir. Art Ligthart, CDT of Y. Digital BV

A Field Guide to Digital Transformation

A Field Guide to Digital Transformation

Thomas Erl
Roger Stoffers

 Pearson

The authors and publisher have taken care in the preparation of this book, but make no expressed or implied warranty of any kind and assume no responsibility for errors or omissions. No liability is assumed for incidental or consequential damages in connection with or arising out of the use of the information or programs contained herein.

Many of the designations used by manufacturers and sellers to distinguish their products are claimed as trademarks. Where those designations appear in this book, and the publisher was aware of a trademark claim, the designations have been printed with initial capital letters or in all capitals.

Cover photo by Thomas Erl; chapter and part opening photos by Nikolas Erl.

For information about buying this title in bulk quantities, or for special sales opportunities (which may include electronic versions; custom cover designs; and content particular to your business, training goals, marketing focus, or branding interests), please contact our corporate sales department at corpsales@pearsoned.com or (800) 382-3419.

For government sales inquiries, please contact governmentsales@pearsoned.com.

For questions about sales outside the U.S., please contact intlcs@pearson.com.

Visit us on the web: informit.com/

Library of Congress Number: 2021947092

Copyright 2022 by Arcitura Education Inc.

ISBN-13: 978-0-13-757184-0
ISBN-10: 0-13-757184-4

Printed and bound by CPI Group (UK) Ltd, Croydon, CR0 4YY

ScoutAutomatedPrintCode

Editor-in-Chief
Mark Taub

Executive Editor
Nancy Davis

Managing Editor
Sandra Schroeder

Senior Project Editor
Lori Lyons

Design/Composition
Kim Scott/Bumpy Design

Copy Editor
María Pareni Barceló
 Nieves

Indexer
James Minkin

Proofreader
Williams Woods
 Publishing Services, LLC

Cover Design
Thomas Erl

Graphics
Kamilla Bieska

Photos
Nikolas Erl

Cover Composition
Chuti Prasertsith

Educational Content Development
Arcitura Education Inc.

To Zuzana, Nikolas and Markus.
Thank you for continually transforming my life.
—Thomas Erl

I would like to dedicate this book to my wife Veronique,
and my children Niels and Nina for their continued support
throughout the authoring and reviewing process,
as it has kept me away from them for significant periods of time.

Also I would like to extend a big thank you to
my family and my friends who still seem to remember me
after emerging from the "book mode."
—Roger Stoffers

Contents at a Glance

Contents

PART I: DIGITAL TRANSFORMATION FUNDAMENTALS

Chapter 11: An Introduction to Digital Transformation Data Science Technologies 171

Chapter 12: Inside a Customer-Centric Solution 193

Acknowledgments

In alphabetical order by last name:

- Ramesh Aki, Staff VP – Digital Platforms and Engineering, Anthem, Inc.

- Matt Armstrong-Barnes, Chief Technologist, Hewlett Packard Enterprise

- Coen de Bruijn, Program Director Data & Analytics, Nike (and Author of "Key Performance Illusions")

- Alex Chizhevsky, PhD., Head of Integration and Data Architecture Practice, Financial Industry

- Mark Cloesmeijer, Co-Founder, Precedence

- Andre Dieball, Director Technical Customer Success DACH

- Jeroen van Disseldorp, CEO, Axual

- Simon Farrugia, Owner and Business & IT Transformation Specialist at BluBox BV

- Edwin van Gorp, Leading Architects

- SunTae Hong, Cloudist

- Jiri Kobelka, CEO, Tatum

- Michael Lambert, Director of Platform Strategy and Application Portfolio Management, Ally

- Art Ligthart, CDT of Y. Digital BV

- Brian Lokhorst, Lead Architect SOA Competence Center, Dutch Tax and Customs Organisation

- Paulo Merson, Brazilian Federal Court of Accounts, Carnegie Mellon University, University of Brasília

- Jan-Willem Middelburg, Managing Director, Cybiant Asia Sdn. Bhd.

- Eric Barceló Monroy, Head of Technology Architecture Consulting, Entra a la Gran Nube, SA de CV

- Amin Naserpour, Founder of TEAM Scorecard

- Thirumurthi Ranganathan, MBA

- Gabriele Rossi, Enterprise Architect, ABN Amro Bank

- Samuel Rostam, Technical Advisor & Adjunct Professor, New York Institute of Technology

- Michel Ruijterman, CIO and Director ITC, de Volksbank

- Khalid Saad, Advisor, Infrastructure Planning, Abu Dhabi Digital Authority

- Morten Stender, PhD, Partner of Staun&Stender

- Hans Tesselaar, Executive Director, Banking Industry Architecture Network (BIAN)

- Dennis E. Wisnosky, Founder the Wizdom Companies, CTO-CA (ret), DoD Business Mission Area

A special thanks to Clemens Utschig (CTO of Boehringer Ingelheim) for his detailed and thoughtful input throughout the authoring process.

Register Your Book

Register your copy of *A Field Guide to Digital Transformation* at informit.com for convenient access to downloads, updates, and corrections as they become available. To start the registration process, go to informit.com/register and log in or create an account. Enter the product ISBN **9780137571840** and click Submit. Once the process is complete, you will find any available bonus content under "Registered Products" for an Access Bonus Content link next to this product, and follow that link to access any available bonus materials. If you would like to be notified of exclusive offers on new editions and updates, please check the box to receive email from us.

About This Book

The purpose of this book is to provide easy-to-understand, plain English coverage of digital transformation and its commonly associated technologies. This preface briefly describes how the chapters in the book are organized, what topics are and are not covered, and an important color convention used in the many diagrams throughout all chapters.

How This Book is Organized

This book is organized into two parts:

- *Part I: Digital Transformation Fundamentals*
- *Part II: Digital Transformation in Practice*

Part I provides simple and clear coverage of basic and essential digital transformation topics. The chapters in this part were deliberately authored with *minimal references to technologies* so that they can be fully understood by both technically and non-technically inclined readers.

Part I contains a set of short chapters that cover the following:

- What is Digital Transformation? (*Chapter 1: Understanding Digital Transformation*)
- What Led to Digital Transformation? (*Chapter 2: Common Business Drivers*)
- What Enables Digital Transformation? (*Chapter 3: Common Technology Drivers*)
- Why Undergo a Digital Transformation? (*Chapter 4: Common Benefits and Goals*
- What Are the Pitfalls of Digital Transformation? (*Chapter 5: Common Risks and Challenges*)

…and Part I continues with three further chapters that establish some basic terms and concepts vital to digital transformation:

- *Chapter 6: Realizing Customer-Centricity*
- *Chapter 7: Data Intelligence Basics*
- *Chapter 8: Intelligent Decision-Making*

The chapters in Part II are focused on describing digital transformation in action. *These chapters are technical, although all coverage of technologies is introductory.*

Part II contains the following four chapters:

- *Chapter 9: Understanding Digital Transformation Solutions*
- *Chapter 10: An Introduction to Digital Transformation Automation Technologies*
- *Chapter 11: An Introduction to Digital Transformation Data Science Technologies*
- *Chapter 12: Inside a Customer-Centric Solution*

While Chapter 9 provides a brief overview of what comprises a digital transformation solution, the next two chapters dive into the primary associated technologies. These chapters provide introductory coverage of each technology individually and also explain how each relates to digital transformation as a whole.

Chapter 12, the final chapter is this book, builds upon and brings together all preceding chapters by providing a detailed, step-by-step exploration of a sample business scenario, as carried out by a customer-centric digital transformation solution.

What This Book Covers

This book provides clear coverage of:

- what digital transformation is and how and when it is applied
- how and why digital transformation emerged
- the business goals and benefits realized by successful digital transformation
- the challenges and risks associated with digital transformation
- the relationship of digital transformation and customer-centricity
- the role and importance of data and data intelligence
- the role and importance of manual and automated decision-making
- primary automation technologies used in digital transformation solutions
- primary data science technologies used in digital transformation solutions
- how a digital transformation solution works
- how a digital transformation solution collects data and uses data intelligence
- how customer-centricity is realized in the real world

What This Book Does Not Cover

While the book does reference and touch on several of the following topics, it does not provide any detailed coverage of:

- digital transformation security considerations
- digital transformation planning guidelines
- how digital transformation impacts an organization's structure and culture
- managing and governing digital transformations
- implementation of automation and data science technologies

Color Convention

Throughout this book, there are diagrams that depict digital transformation solutions, as well as organizations that are undergoing digital transformation. To better distinguish these parts of the diagrams, a standard blue color is used for associated symbols, as shown in Figure A.

Figure A

The blue color shown is used for symbols that represent participants in digital transformation. This can include organizations, solutions, humans, technologies, products, etc.

Furthermore, transition arrows are often used to show how scenarios progress or to compare "before" and "after" type scenarios, as shown in Figure B.

Figure B

If the "after" scenario demonstrates the application of digital transformation, then a blue transition arrow is used (top). If the diagram depicts a transition that does not involve digital transformation, then a grey arrow is used instead (bottom).

> **NOTE**
>
> Often a distinction is made between digital transformation and *digital optimization*. The latter term can be used when the goal is primarily to improve existing business operations, products and services. When a business intends to digitally *transform*, the goal is often to also introduce new models into the business and launch new products and services. For the sake of simplicity, only the term digital transformation is used in this book.

Introducing "CC," your Field Guide

As explained and demonstrated throughout this book, customer-centricity is at the heart of digital transformation. Improving how organizations make and maintain positive customer connections is often a primary motivation behind investing in digital transformations.

A part of realizing customer-centricity is making the customer experience as warm and accessible as possible. To put this into practice, this book introduces a character named "CC" who acts as your friendly guide to the field of digital transformation (Figure C). "CC" will appear periodically to highlight and summarize key topics.

I'll be your guide!

Figure C
"CC" will provide some helpful guidance along your journey into digital transformation.

Part I

Digital Transformation Fundamentals

Chapter 1

Understanding Digital Transformation (What is Digital Transformation?)

Business, Technology, Data and People

Please prepare yourself. We are about to... "transform".

Let's start by establishing the overall purpose and scope of digital transformation. In this chapter we learn how business, technology, data and people must all align for a harmonious transformation.

A digital transformation initiative is a genuine attempt to change, upgrade and extend an organization's business models and technologies so as to enable the organization to:

- gain value by significantly improving what it has been doing

- gain value by introducing new things it can do (and to ensure it can do those new things really well)

A digital transformation can introduce:

- a new mindset

- a new culture

- a new organizational structure

- new priorities

- new technologies

- new risks and challenges

A digital transformation will impact an organization's:

- business models and processes

- automation and data science technologies

- human workers and culture

Specifically, the mainstream availability of a specific set of technology innovations and practices has enabled organizations to transform their businesses through enhanced automation and data intelligence to achieve greater business value and growth. This transformation results in changes to organizational culture and the positioning and allocation of human workers.

The upcoming chapters explore the business and technology drivers that led to the emergence of mainstream digital transformation, as well as the common goals, benefits, risks and challenges of digitally transforming an organization. But first, this chapter takes a closer look at what fundamentally comprises digital transformation.

Business, Technology, Data and People

Although technology innovations are responsible for enabling digital transformation, the motivations, impacts, and influences of an organization's digital transformation effort go well beyond technology (Figure 1.1). As explained in the upcoming sections, these factors involve the organization's business, its data and its people.

Figure 1.1
A digital transformation involves four primary factors: business, technology, data and people.

> **NOTE**
>
> Within the context of digital transformation and throughout this book, the term *business* represents the purpose, mission and/or the primary activities carried out by an organization. The term applies to for-profit and not-for-profit organizations in any industry.
>
> Another key term used in this book is *data intelligence*, which is data that is of value to the organization and is relevant and meaningful to the organization's business. Data intelligence is extracted from data, meaning that a quantity of (raw or general) data is processed and filtered to generate a subset of data that provides intelligence (useful information) to the organization and its business.
>
> Much of digital transformation is focused on the creation and utilization of data intelligence. While data is shown as one of the four primary factors in Figure 1.1, it is implied that it is data intelligence (meaningful data) that provides the benefits indicated in Figures 1.2, 1.5 and 1.6.

Digital Transformation and Business

Digital transformation is a genuine attempt to take an organization's business to a new level of growth and effectiveness by transforming:

- how the business relates to the outside world (in particular, how customers perceive and inter-relate with the business), and…

- how the business operates internally (in particular, how different organizational departments may need to collaborate, and how humans and machines may need to collaborate and inter-relate with each other).

When successfully realized, digital transformation can significantly reshape and enhance many aspects of an organization's business, including:

- the extent to which the business can make existing products and services available to new customers and new markets

- the extent to which the business can introduce new products and services into new markets

- the speed at which the business can penetrate and develop new markets

- the extent to which the business can leverage data

- the experience that customers have when interacting with the business

- the efficiency with which the business can operate and the level of automation the business can incorporate

- the agility with which the business can maneuver and adapt to change

- the manner in which the business can collaborate with partners

A common, overarching strategic goal of digital business transformation is to instill customer-centricity as being paramount to business models, automation and the organizational culture.

A successful digital business transformation (including the attainment of a meaningful extent of enhanced customer-centricity) is enabled by the successful application of contemporary technology and data intelligence, along with the successful contributions of human workers (Figure 1.2).

Figure 1.2

The business improvements and the introduction of new lines of business are enabled by human workers and automation technology, and further enhanced by increased data intelligence.

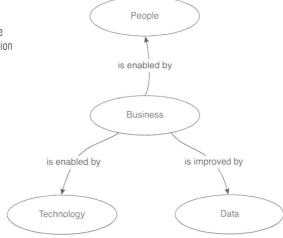

Digital Transformation and Technology

What has made digital transformation possible is a set of technology innovations that enable organizations to carry out significant and meaningful business transformations.

The primary distinguishing automation technologies are:

- Cloud Computing
- Blockchain
- Internet of Things (IoT)
- Robotic Process Automation (RPA)

The primary distinguishing data science technologies are:

- Big Data Analysis and Analytics
- Machine Learning
- Artificial Intelligence (AI)

TIP
We won't be mentioning these technologies much in Part I of this book. We'll start exploring them in Part II.

Together, these technology innovations empower business capabilities in two primary areas:

- improved and new forms of automation
- more meaningful and responsive data intelligence

An organization's business requirements and goals in relation to its planned digital transformation will help determine the correct combination of these technologies.

While the chapters in Part I of this book make occasional references to these technologies, much of Part II is dedicated to describing the technologies and exploring how they can be positioned as part of digital transformation solutions and platforms (Figure 1.3).

Figure 1.3
The icons used in the chapters in Part II of this book to represent the primary digital transformation technologies. From left to right: Cloud Computing, Blockchain, Internet of Things (IoT), Robotic Process Automation (RPA), Big Data, Machine Learning and Artificial Intelligence (AI).

The utilization of these technologies is driven by the requirements of the business, and they correspondingly generate and process data in support of business data intelligence requirements. Human workers can be further supported by the digital transformation solutions resulting from the application of these technologies. In some cases, the new capabilities introduced by the solutions may allow manual tasks carried out by human workers to be automated by the solutions (Figure 1.4).

Figure 1.4
The utilization of technology innovations is determined by the new business requirements, which also determine how new automation technology relates to human workers. New technology innovations further introduce the capabilities necessary to create, collect and process new data in order to produce meaningful data intelligence.

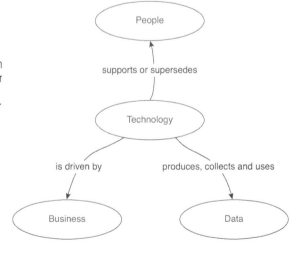

Digital Transformation and Data

Digital transformation leads to automated business processes that are naturally data-driven. Data becomes a prime asset that empowers the organization to develop sophisticated business automation.

The utilization of contemporary data science technologies as part of a digital transformation can inject an organization with large quantities of "data intelligence," meaning the organization will have the opportunity to:

- gain meaningful insights into its own operations

- gain meaningful insights into its market or community

- gain meaningful insights into customer history and behavior

- gain meaningful insights into its existing products and services

- discover opportunities to introduce new products and services into its market or community

- enable its systems to learn from historical data to produce improved analysis results

- enable its systems to assume decision-making responsibilities

Data intelligence can be used to improve automation and increase opportunities to automate manual tasks previously carried out by human workers. Data intelligence can further support human workers responsible for carrying out decisions (Figure 1.5).

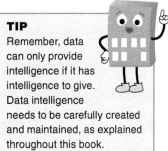

TIP
Remember, data can only provide intelligence if it has intelligence to give. Data intelligence needs to be carefully created and maintained, as explained throughout this book.

Figure 1.5

The infusion of deeply meaningful and
insightful data enables automation solutions,
human workers and the organization itself to
carry out business more intelligently.

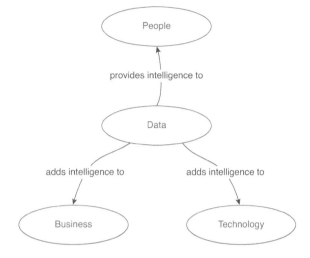

Digital Transformation and People

The transformation of both business and technology landscapes within an organization
will naturally augment or reshape traditional organizational structures and change the
way human workers contribute and relate to the organization.

For example:

- Sophisticated new technologies can automate a range of tasks that have historically been carried out manually by human workers.

- Human workers that previously performed menial tasks that are automated
  can now be retrained and reallocated to carry out more challenging and
  meaningful tasks.

- Human workers with new skill-sets are required to implement and maintain new
  automation technologies and, in particular, new data science technologies.

- The introduction of data intelligence as part of digital transformation solutions
  and as part of enhanced or new business operations can introduce the need for
  new knowledge and skill development, both in terms of producing and utilizing
  the data intelligence.

- Human workers affected by changes to business models and business processes
  may need to be retrained and perhaps even acquire new skills.

- The introduction of new products and services can introduce the need to hire new human workers capable of operating within the new supporting business processes.

All of these changes to how human workers carry out new or improved business tasks, work with new technology, learn from new data intelligence and collaborate and relate to the organization in new ways (Figure 1.6), can lead to the formation of new organizational cultures, more integrated with digital capabilities and focused on customer-centricity.

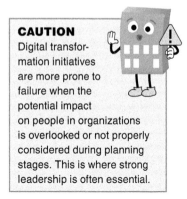

CAUTION Digital transformation initiatives are more prone to failure when the potential impact on people in organizations is overlooked or not properly considered during planning stages. This is where strong leadership is often essential.

Figure 1.6
Human workers can be empowered to carry out the business more effectively via the availability of new automation technology and data intelligence.

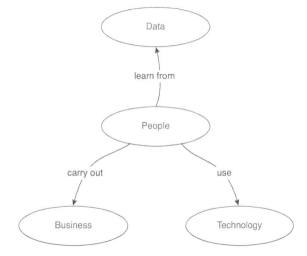

Digital Transformation and Organizations and Solutions

As previously established, an organization undergoing a digital transformation will inevitably introduce benefits and impose challenges on its business operations, its technology ecosystem, the utilization of its data, as well as its relationships with its human workers (Figure 1.7).

To proceed with a digital transformation, the organization will need to develop *digital transformation solutions*, which are essentially applications responsible for automating and/or contributing data intelligence, each of which may encompass one or more related business tasks.

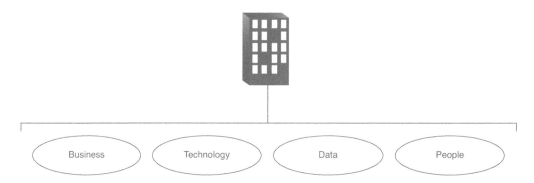

Figure 1.7
An organization's transformation relates to and impacts its business, technology, data and people.

An organization will typically end up building multiple digital transformation solutions that share resources, such as infrastructure and databases as part of a greater platform (Figure 1.8).

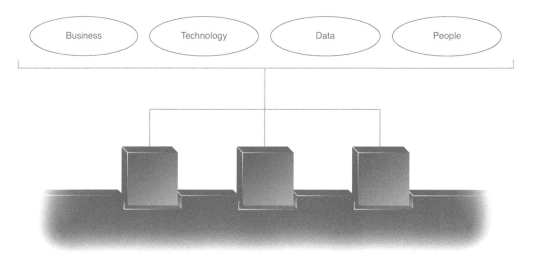

Figure 1.8
The introduction of digital transformation solutions enables an organization to carry out its new business transformation requirements via new technologies capable of producing and processing new data intelligence. Digital transformation solutions will further change how and where people within the organization contribute to business operations.

Chapter 2

Common Business Drivers
(What Led to Digital Transformation?)

Losing Touch with Customer Communities

Inability to Grow in Stale Marketplaces

Inability to Adapt to Rapidly Changing Marketplaces

Cold Customer Relationships

Inefficient Operations

Inefficient Decision-Making

Let's now go over some of the common business problems that can be fixed with a successful digital transformation. If your organization can relate to any of the problems described in this chapter, it just might mean that it's time for a "renovation."

The best starting point to better understanding digital transformation is learning about the reasons that led to its emergence. This brief chapter covers key business drivers, each of which describes a common business problem that organizations have been facing and that is addressed by digital transformation.

The following key business drivers are covered:

- Losing Touch with Customer Communities

- Inability to Grow in Stale Marketplaces

- Inability to Adapt to Rapidly Changing Marketplaces

- Cold Customer Relationships

- Inefficient Operations

- Inefficient Decision-Making

Losing Touch with Customer Communities

With most services and products being available online, it is easier than ever for customers to browse and discover new options and alternatives. Furthermore, customer communities are themselves becoming more sophisticated with online and social technology. The overall evolution of customer communities has raised expectation levels with business vendors, while lowering their tolerance of more traditional business approaches.

This has negatively impacted many organizations that are unable to respond to or keep up with these raised expectations. Such organizations can lose market share as a result of losing touch with customer communities they previously established (Figure 2.1).

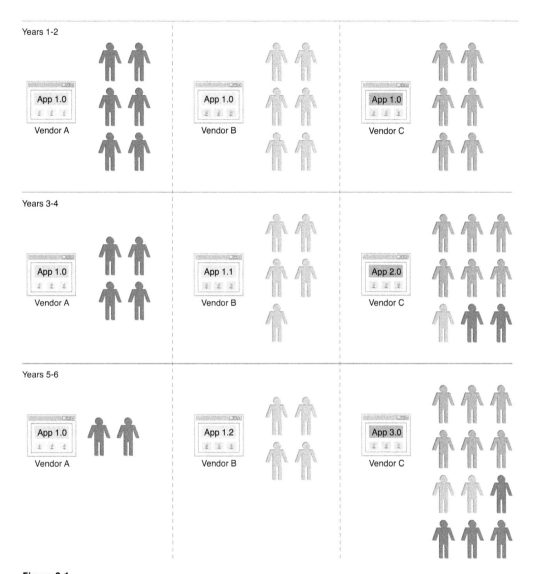

Figure 2.1

Vendor A does not change its online applications as the years go by while Vendor B only changes its applications incrementally. Vendor C makes an effort to significantly upgrade and transform the products and services available via its online applications on a regular basis, thereby allowing it to lure more customers away from Vendors A and B.

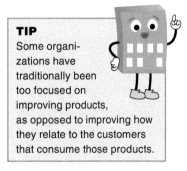

TIP

Some organizations have traditionally been too focused on improving products, as opposed to improving how they relate to the customers that consume those products.

Digital transformation can enable organizations to recognize and respond to customer community trends. Digital transformation platforms and solutions are typically designed to be customer-centric from the ground up, allowing businesses to gain competitive advantages by improving their online presence to continue to meet and exceed customer expectations.

Inability to Grow in Stale Marketplaces

For years, several marketplaces did not change because businesses established themselves as the primary suppliers in those markets and, from a customer's perspective, there was little to distinguish one from the other (Figure 2.2). This has stalled the growth of some organizations while completely inhibiting the growth of others.

The enhanced data intelligence used in digital transformation solutions and the manner in which such solutions are designed with the primary goals of improving customer experience and introducing new innovations can help organizations break away from (or break into) a stale marketplace to noticeably distinguish themselves from competitors.

Inability to Adapt to Rapidly Changing Marketplaces

In more volatile marketplaces, change is a constant factor. Vendors may aggressively introduce new, unique products or services or impose new promotions that are difficult to compete with. Organizations in such business climates can find themselves outmatched, especially when their competitors are larger and wealthier.

Other factors that can introduce rapid change into marketplaces can be political or regulatory influences that can affect international trading or currencies. These too can lead to volatile marketplaces.

As international communities become more connected and responsive, corresponding marketplaces may be subject to greater and more rapid change. Organizations without the ability to adapt to such changes can find themselves left behind (Figure 2.3).

Figure 2.2

The customer browses several online stores to decide from which it will purchase a specific set of grocery and beauty items. Other than price and shipping options, the customer sees little difference between what the online vendors have to offer.

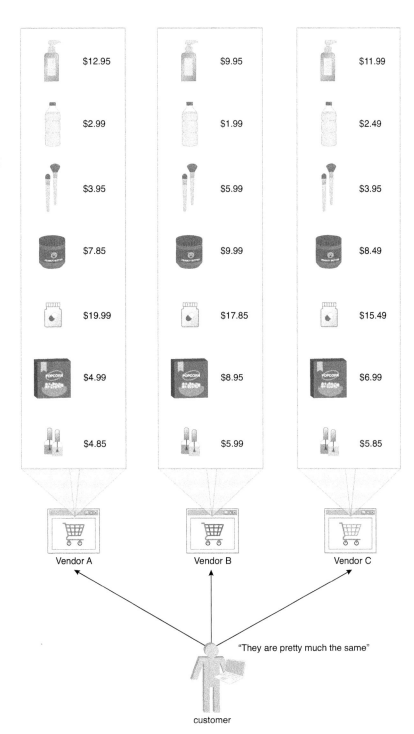

Figure 2.3

While Vendors B and C offer the range of products they normally do, Vendor A has begun innovating by offering a wider range of new products, making it difficult for the other vendors to compete.

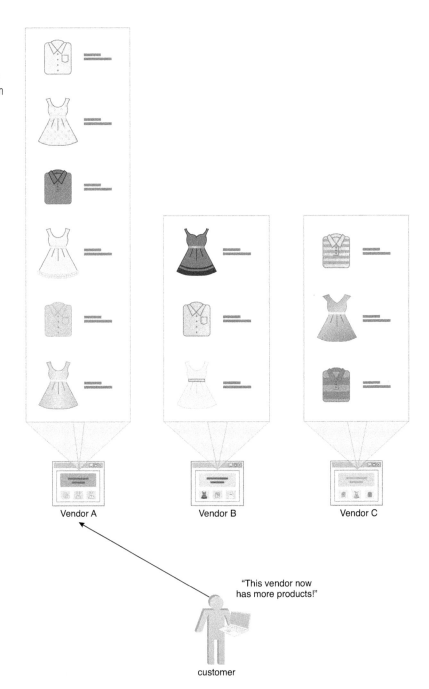

Digital transformation can intrinsically improve an organization's ability to act more responsively to unforeseen change, such as rapid developments in business marketplaces. Digital transformation especially supports aggressive innovation, such as to enable organizations to introduce new, disruptive products and services into a marketplace.

Cold Customer Relationships

On a fundamental level, many organizations establish relatively impersonal relationships with their customers. Customer dissatisfaction has remained common in every industry for decades (Figure 2.4). Many private and public organizations have recognized that there is much benefit to building "warm," long-lasting relationships with their client communities. However, though the desire has been there, there has traditionally been little innovation in this field that has supported the development of truly customer-centric automation solutions.

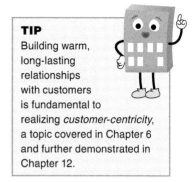

TIP
Building warm, long-lasting relationships with customers is fundamental to realizing *customer-centricity*, a topic covered in Chapter 6 and further demonstrated in Chapter 12.

Digital transformation provides a genuine opportunity for an organization to dramatically improve customer satisfaction for the purposes of building longer term relationships with existing customers and attracting new customers.

Inefficient Operations

While most organizations already utilize business automation technology to automate various parts of their operations, the extent of automation is often limited to those tasks that are obvious automation candidates and for which the development of automation systems is relatively straight-forward. Many menial steps in modern operational workflows therefore remain dependent on human involvement, which can result in on-going performance limitations (Figure 2.5).

Digital transformation solutions can introduce technologies that can more easily and effectively automate tasks that have been commonly carried out manually.

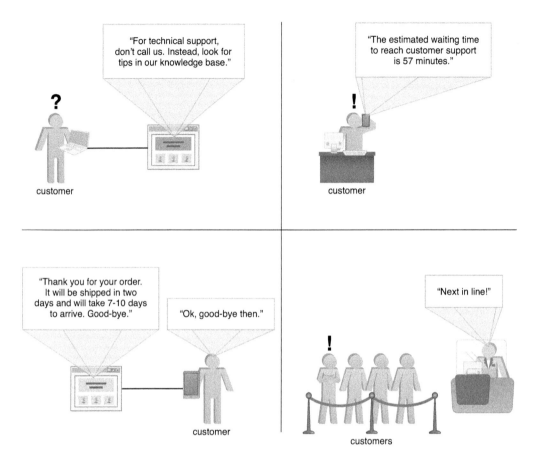

Figure 2.4

Traditional ways in which businesses interact with customers can be relatively "cold" in that little or no effort is made to improve the customer experience.

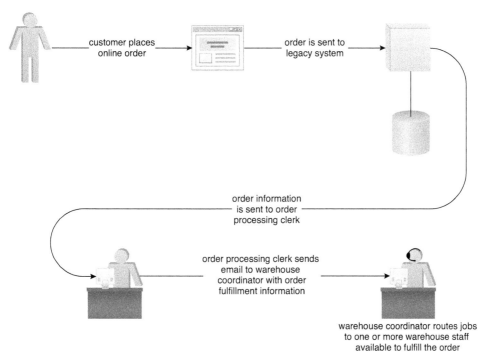

Figure 2.5
Although the collection and recording of customer orders are automated, the subsequent processing and order fulfillment assignment tasks continue to be carried out manually.

Inefficient Decision-Making

Even for organizations that already have significant automation solutions powering their day-to-day operations, they traditionally continue to rely upon key personnel to make the majority of operational decisions.

Many repetitive decisions made by humans are based on simple decision-making criteria. Other decisions made by humans are based on decision-making criteria too complex for a human to process efficiently. In either case, the involvement of a human decision maker can lead to unnecessarily inefficient operations (Figure 2.6).

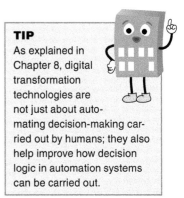

TIP
As explained in Chapter 8, digital transformation technologies are not just about automating decision-making carried out by humans; they also help improve how decision logic in automation systems can be carried out.

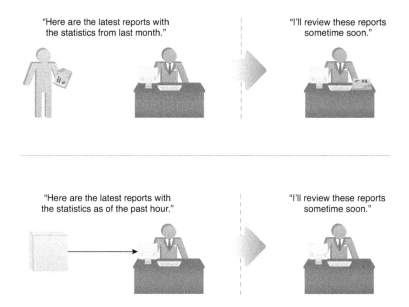

Figure 2.6

The rate at which reporting data is provided to decision makers and the time it takes humans to make decisions can be insufficiently slow to keep up with market demands.

Digital transformation platforms introduce a sophisticated level of data intelligence, as well as data-driven systems that can use this data intelligence to automate a range of decisions that have customarily been carried out by humans.

Chapter 3

Common Technology Drivers
(What Enables Digital Transformation?)

Enhanced and Diverse Data Collection

Contemporary Data Science

Sophisticated Automation Technology

Autonomous Decision-Making

Centralized, Scalable, Resilient IT Resources

Immutable Data Storage

Ubiquitous Multiexperience Access

Let's now highlight some of the useful technologies that drove digital transformation into the IT mainstream. Organizations often need an open mind to fully comprehend how and to what extent the capabilities provided by these technologies can support their business goals.

As established in Chapter 1, the availability of a specific set of technology innovations has made digital transformation possible. This chapter explains how these technologies have acted as the primary enablers of digital transformation.

The following key technology drivers are covered:

- Enhanced and Diverse Data Collection

- Contemporary Data Science

- Sophisticated Automation Technology

- Autonomous Decision-Making

- Centralized, Scalable, Resilient IT Resources

- Immutable Data Storage

- Ubiquitous Multiexperience Access

NOTE
The chapters in Part II of this book provide introductory coverage of the digital transformation technologies relevant to the technology drivers described in this chapter. Chapter 9, in particular, maps the seven key digital transformation technologies to these technology drivers.

Enhanced and Diverse Data Collection

Digital transformation platforms encompass technology innovations capable of collecting an extremely broad range of diverse data.

For example:

- Customer-centric solution design and associated monitoring technology can capture a great deal of customer profile and behavioral data from how and when customers interact with an organization's existing applications.

- Solutions can encompass a network of remote sensors capable of collecting and streaming large quantities of telemetry data from the outside world, including human activity, vehicle activity, transport logistics, weather, vibration and many activities associated with electronic devices.

- Third-party market data can be acquired and processed through data analytics solutions that can extract meaningful insights into individuals and entire communities.

- Paper-based documents can be digitized to provide a greater archive of input data which the organization can further subject to analysis and processing in conjunction with other input data.

By having such a wide range of data as input, digital transformation platforms can:

- offer human decision makers deeply insightful data intelligence to help improve their decision-making capabilities and to further help them discover how new product and service innovations could be introduced

- perform highly sophisticated and intelligent forms of automation that can improve both the quality and efficiency of how business is automated (Figure 3.1)

- enable the opportunity to automate decision-making responsibilities as part of digital transformation automation solutions (as discussed separately in *Chapter 8: Intelligent Decision-Making*)

However the collected data is utilized, data intelligence that remains meaningful and is constantly accumulating can become an extremely valuable asset to the organization.

TIP
So, where does the data come from and how is it collected? This is all explained in *Chapter 7: Data Intelligence Basics.*

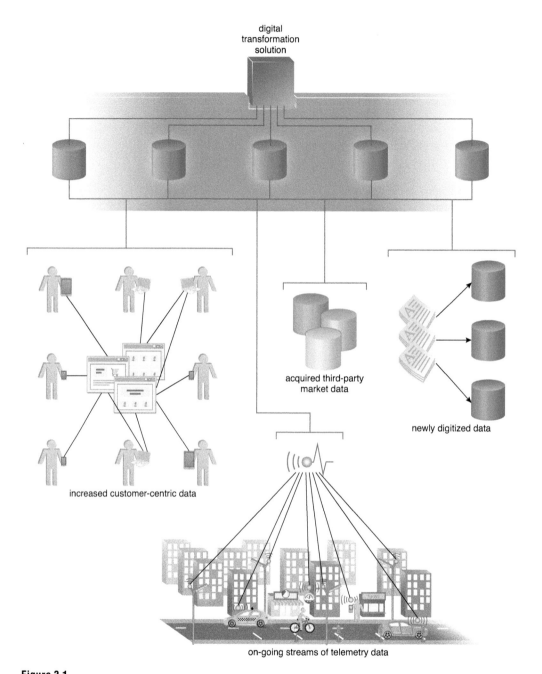

Figure 3.1
A digital transformation solution may access and utilize data that was collected from a wide variety of sources. This enables the solution to perform its functions more effectively and to further improve how it performs its functions over time.

> **NOTE**
>
> Technologies relevant to this driver include:
>
> - Big Data Analysis and Analytics
> - Internet of Things (IoT)
> - Robotic Process Automation (RPA)
>
> These technologies are described in Chapters 10 and 11.

Contemporary Data Science

The ability to collect large quantities of data is only of benefit if the data can be correctly processed, filtered and analyzed to be of relevance and value to the organization and its automation solutions.

Data science practices and technologies that have traditionally been fringe parts of the IT industry have become part of the IT mainstream and lie at the heart of digital transformation environments.

For example, these data science technologies can be used to:

- consolidate, process and filter large volumes of diverse data so as to produce meaningful and relevant analysis results

- process and learn from a constant stream of input data so as to produce increasingly sophisticated analysis results (Figure 3.2)

- enable solutions to carry out autonomous decision-making

> **CAUTION**
>
> As powerful as contemporary data science technology is, its actual value to an organization is dependent on the proficiency of those responsible for implementing it correctly.

Contemporary data science advances are what have propelled digital transformation automation into many organizations, as their automation solutions can now be driven by constant streams of intelligent data that provide genuine value.

> **NOTE**
>
> Technologies relevant to this driver include:
>
> - Big Data Analysis and Analytics
> - Machine Learning
> - Artificial Intelligence (AI)
>
> These technologies are described in Chapter 11.

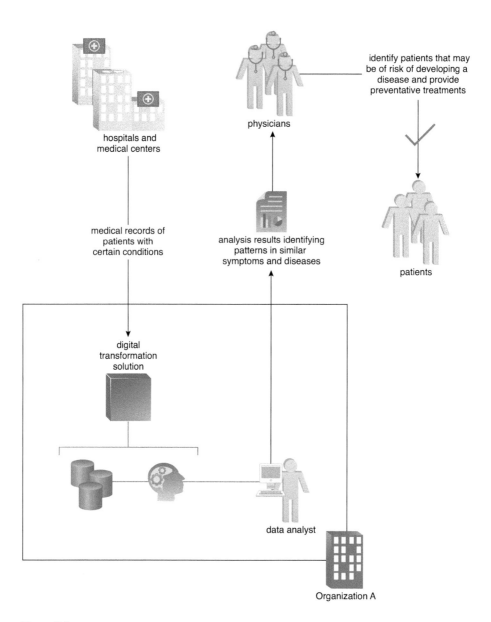

Figure 3.2

Medical records provided by hospitals and medical centers are used by physicians to help identify patterns that assist in diagnosing patients with similar conditions or predicting the likelihood of such conditions developing.

Sophisticated Automation Technology

Manual tasks that have traditionally not been easily auto-mated can now be fully automated. Special software pro-grams called "bots" can be configured to carry out a range of hands-on processing tasks, such as data entry and infor-mation routing (Figure 3.3). The behavior and functionality of bots can be further enhanced through the use of data science technologies.

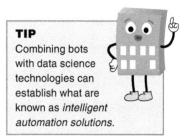

TIP
Combining bots with data science technologies can establish what are known as *intelligent automation solutions*.

> **NOTE**
>
> The technology primarily relevant to this benefit is Robotic Process Auto-mation (RPA), as described in Chapter 10.

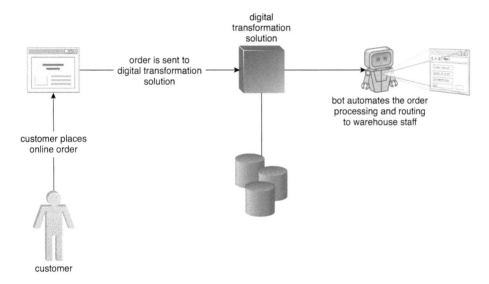

digital transformation solution

order is sent to digital transformation solution

bot automates the order processing and routing to warehouse staff

customer places online order

customer

Figure 3.3
A software program known as a "bot" is given the responsibility to complete order processing-related tasks that were previously carried out by humans.

Autonomous Decision-Making

Modern digital transformation solutions can incorporate data science technologies that can assume decision-making responsibilities. This enables the solution to rapidly respond to a range of situations that may have previously required more time for cor-rect human decisions to be carried out (Figure 3.4).

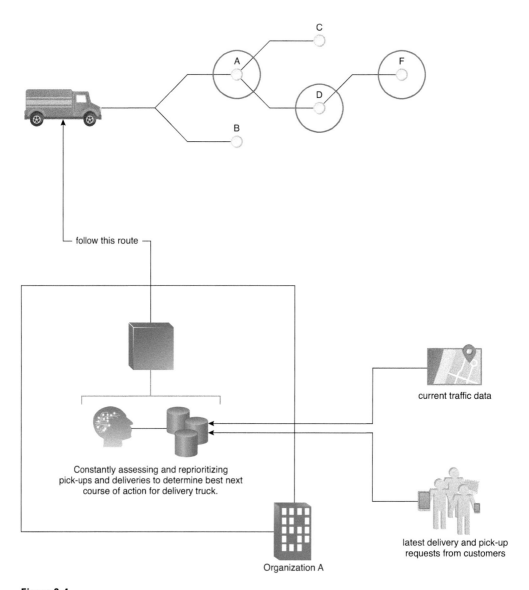

Figure 3.4

A digital transformation solution dynamically determines the route a delivery truck should take to visit the warehouses where deliveries are to be transported. The system takes into account current traffic data and current customer request data.

This type of solution can further be designed to process and learn from past decisions it carried out so that it can assess itself in order to continually improve its own decision-making capabilities.

> **NOTE**
>
> The technology primarily relevant to this benefit is Artificial Intelligence (AI), as described in Chapter 11.

Centralized, Scalable, Resilient IT Resources

Digital transformation solutions commonly have distinct performance requirements, such as:

- high scalability to accommodate large quantities of concurrent users

- dynamic scalability to accommodate unpredictable usage fluctuations

- high resiliency to recover from failure with minimal disruptions in service

- high compute power to process large quantities of data

- rapid provisioning of new solutions and solution updates

- centralized IT resources that can be shared by multiple solutions

Cloud-based environments can provide the necessary infrastructure to support these and other digital transformation solution performance requirements. Such environments can be established within the organization or they can be leased from third-party providers. Organizations can also have their own private cloud that can automatically scale out to an external third-party cloud, when the processing limitations of the private cloud are exceeded (Figure 3.5).

> **TIP**
>
> Public cloud providers typically offer "pay-as-you-go" pricing so that you only pay for your actual usage of their IT resources.

> **NOTE**
>
> The technology primarily relevant to this benefit is Cloud Computing, as described in Chapter 10.

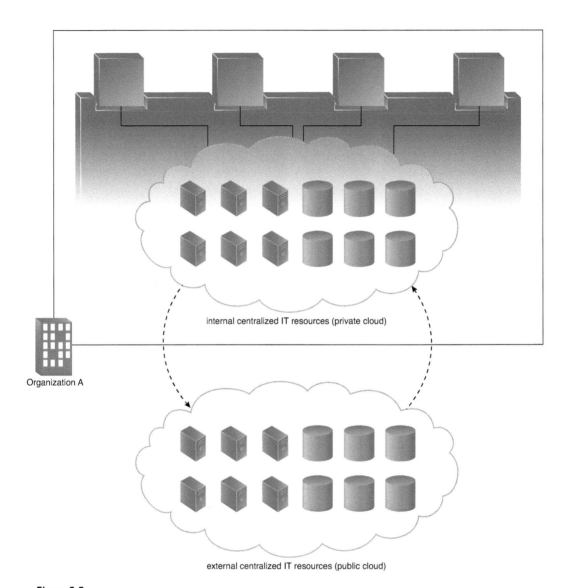

Figure 3.5

An organization can centralize IT resources into a private cloud that it owns and operates internally. It can further opt to balance or "burst-out" to additional IT resources residing in a public cloud, when necessary.

Immutable Data Storage

With the increase in the quantity of digital data being collected, there is a greater need for sensitive and important
data to be permanently stored in such a manner that it can
never be altered or manipulated. Highly secure storage
technology that emerged from the use of cryptocurrencies
has made it possible to position immutable repositories
alongside corporate databases, as part of digital transformation solutions (Figure 3.6).

CAUTION
Although immu-
table data storage
repositories are
extremely secure,
they are techno-
logically quite unique and can
be challenging to integrate
with other technologies.

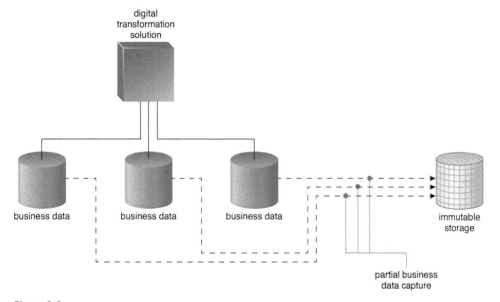

Figure 3.6
A digital transformation solution submits important business records to a repository capable of immutable storage.

NOTE
The technology primarily relevant to this benefit is Blockchain, as described in Chapter 10.

Ubiquitous Multiexperience Access

A key objective when designing customer-centric digital transformation solutions is to provide "multiexperience" support by enabling ubiquitous access to a range of business interaction options (or *channels*) that that the customer can choose from (Figure 3.7). The *Single vs. Multi vs. Omni-Channel Customer Interactions* section in Chapter 6 provides examples of multiexperience access methods.

TIP
The more channels an organization has, the more opportunities it opens up for customers to connect and remain connected.

The utilization of cloud-based environments, along with other technologies, makes it possible to support multiple access channels whereby the "state" of the customer's activity is always preserved across the different access method types. For example, a customer may start a transaction online using a tablet, and can then (at a later point) switch to a voice-activated device to complete the transaction.

NOTE
The technology primarily relevant to this benefit is Cloud Computing, as described in Chapter 10.

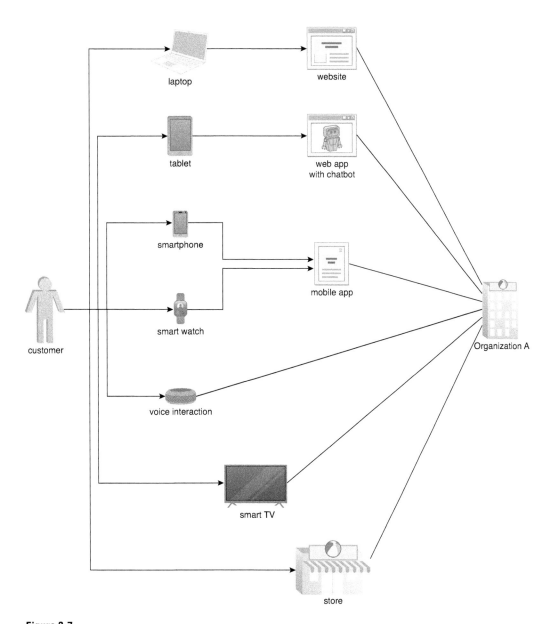

Figure 3.7

A customer may choose to interact with a business using any number of access methods or channels. The business is able to maintain the state of the customer interaction from one channel to the other. For example, the customer might start a transaction using a mobile app and then complete the transaction when visiting the store in person.

Chapter 4

Common Benefits and Goals (Why Undergo a Digital Transformation?)

Enhanced Business Alignment

Enhanced Automation and Productivity

Enhanced Data Intelligence and Decision-Making

Improved Customer Experience and Customer Confidence

Improved Organizational Agility

Improved Ability to Attain Market Growth

*Now comes the fun part. We get to learn about the many
positive things a digital transformation can bring. Organizations
undergoing digital transformation often look forward to
"shaking things up" in their markets and communities.*

The best starting point for assessing the value proposition of a digital transformation initiative is to understand the benefits and goals commonly associated with successful digital transformation efforts. These benefits and goals need to be married with the organization's own business goals so as to determine:

- when (or whether) an organization should invest in and commit to digital transformation

- to what extent the organization should carry out digital transformation

- the rate at which the organization should transform

This chapter begins by summarizing the following primary organizational benefits that result from an organization's successful digital business transformation and the corresponding competency it needs to gain in the automation and data science technologies associated with the previously described technology drivers:

- Enhanced Business Alignment

- Enhanced Automation and Productivity

- Enhanced Data Intelligence and Decision-Making

The chapter then continues by explaining the strategic goals that can be attained by applying the enhancements and capabilities the organization gains from the previously described benefits:

TIP
Realizing key benefits is what helps attain key goals.

- Improved Customer Experience and Customer Confidence

- Improved Organizational Agility

- Improved Ability to Attain Market Growth

Digital transformation results in business and technology enhancements that lead to improvements that help attain goals.

Enhanced Business Alignment

Traditionally, organizations were often structured around business silos based on specific products, services or lines of business.

A digital transformation can introduce the need for:

- previously isolated or separated business departments to collaborate in support of common business goals (Figure 4.1)

- previously separated business and IT departments to collaborate more closely in support of common business goals

- existing business processes and models to be optimized, reengineered and/or further innovated in support of new business goals

- single-purpose business processes previously focused on specific products to be consolidated with others in support of new business goals (Figure 4.2)

- new business processes and models to be introduced and merged with existing business processes and models in support of new business goals (Figures 4.1 and 4.2)

These business transformations and the resulting cross-departmental collaborations that are formed naturally align the business of an organization with its strategic business goals, several of which may be focused on improving customer-centricity.

CAUTION
The actual benefits of rethinking and combining business processes will relate directly to the quality of the newly designed business process. The goal is to consolidate and streamline, but there is always the danger of a new workflow becoming overly complex or convoluted.

This type of business alignment can strengthen an organization culturally, but primarily benefits the organization by establishing a solid foundation upon which automation and data science technology enhancements can be applied. These technologies can be effectively utilized by human workers to enable the organization to realize its business goals to their full potential.

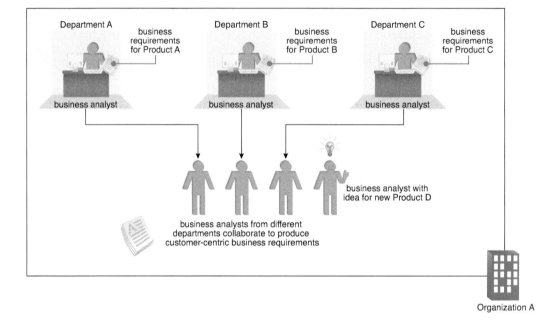

Figure 4.1

A common goal of digital transformation initiatives is to eliminate product "silos" so as to establish an environment that fosters collaboration and alignment across departments. For example, to improve customer-centricity, those groups or departments originally responsible for business analysis as it pertained to individual products, now work together to provide a consolidated customer experience through which all products (and new products) can be explored. New, broader performance and customer success metrics and indicators are commonly established to measure the collective outcome of these types of collaborations instead of measuring only the performance of individual contributions.

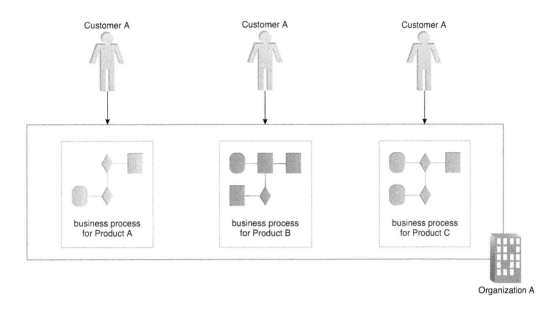

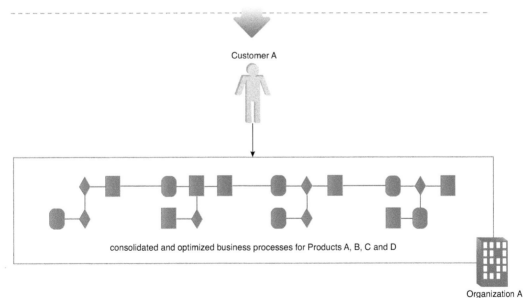

Figure 4.2

Customer A wants to obtain three different products from Organization A. Previously, Customer A had to interact with Organization A via three separate workflows and systems (top), which may have even required the creation of three individual accounts. A transition toward a customer-centric solution results in a consolidated customer experience enabling Customer A to carry out transactions in relation to the three products in a single environment (bottom). Customer A is further able to discover new products while in the consolidated environment.

Enhanced Automation and Productivity

An organization undergoing a digital transformation can extend the reach and improve the quality of its automation capabilities significantly. Solutions can be built using combinations of technologies that can enable organizations to automate business tasks so as to boost operational productivity.

For example, automation technologies can:

- automate tasks that previously needed to be performed manually
- automate new tasks in support of new products and services
- automate data collection across environments outside of organization boundaries
- automate actuating tasks in remote devices outside of organization boundaries
- automate tasks at a higher usage capacity than what was previously achievable
- automate tasks more reliably than what was previously possible
- automate decision-making
- improve the security and quality of storage for private, sensitive and important business data

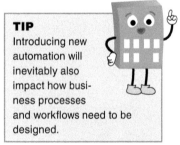

TIP
Introducing new automation will inevitably also impact how business processes and workflows need to be designed.

What is significant about digital transformation environments is how they combine these technologies into distinct platforms that help achieve strategic goals via their collective features (Figure 4.3).

NOTE

Technologies relevant to this benefit are covered in *Chapter 10: An Introduction to Digital Transformation Automation Technologies.*

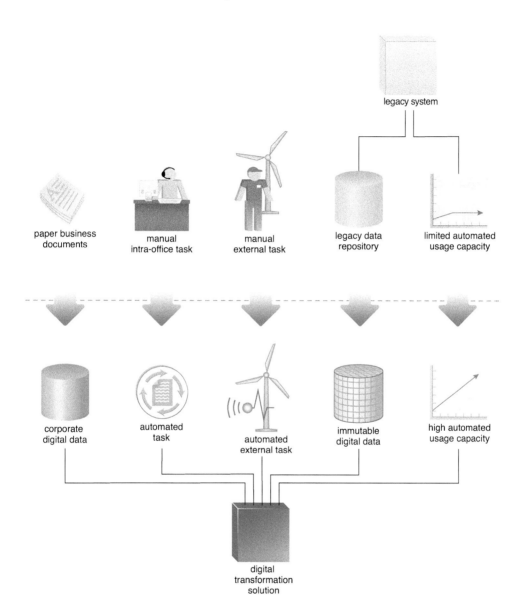

Figure 4.3
The application of digital transformation technology improves the quality and efficiency of a range of operational business tasks.

Enhanced Data Intelligence and Decision-Making

As previously explained, digital transformation solutions can accumulate valuable data intelligence, enabling them to produce deeply insightful analysis results in realtime or near-realtime. This can significantly empower organizations with new insights, new ideas and more decisive and successful decision-making capabilities.

> **TIP**
>
> Much of what constitutes a successful digital transformation relies on the successful attainment of this benefit.

Organizations further have the option to defer some decision-making responsibilities to the underlying digital transformation solutions themselves. When doing so, decisions can be made and executed at the same rate (realtime or near-realtime) as that of the data processing (Figure 4.4).

> **NOTE**
>
> Technologies relevant to this benefit are covered in *Chapter 11: An Introduction to Digital Transformation Data Science Technologies.*

Improved Customer Experience and Customer Confidence

One of the foundational objectives of digital transformation is to foster a shift toward establishing a customer-centric culture, resulting in improved relationships with customers, attracting new customers and supporting all of this via enhanced automation.

Customer-centric solutions have the potential of capturing the interest and enhancing the satisfaction and confidence of customers.

This brings with it several core benefits, including:

- increasing the speed at which customers are served by reducing the time-to-value of services

- improving the effectiveness with which services are delivered to customers by enhancing their quality

- increasing the "warmth" of the customer experience

- improving customer confidence and loyalty by maintaining on-going relationships with customers beyond individual transactions

Digital transformation solutions aim to achieve these improvements by being designed, from the ground up, with customer-centricity in mind (Figure 4.5), as further explored in *Chapter 6: Realizing Customer-Centricity.*

TIP
When we use the term "customer" we are not just referring to business customers. A customer can be any user, employee or client of an organization, whether the organization is a for-profit business or a non-profit or public organization.

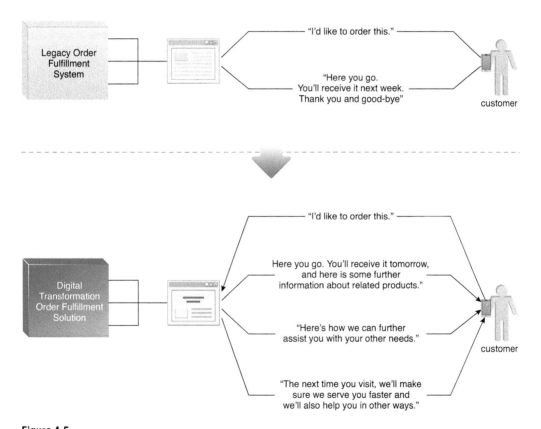

Figure 4.5
Digital transformation solutions are designed to be customer-centric so as to enable customers to interact with an organization in new ways and to make the customers' experiences as positive and effective as possible.

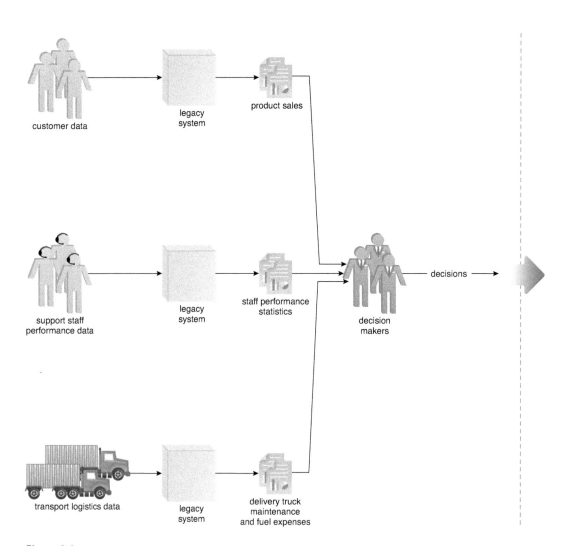

Figure 4.4

Traditional legacy systems produce various independent reports for human decision makers. Digital transformation solutions process and consolidate input data from a range of sources with the aim of producing enhanced reports at a faster rate and with greater data intelligence. The reported data may be provided to human decision makers or to data science systems that can make and act upon decisions autonomously.

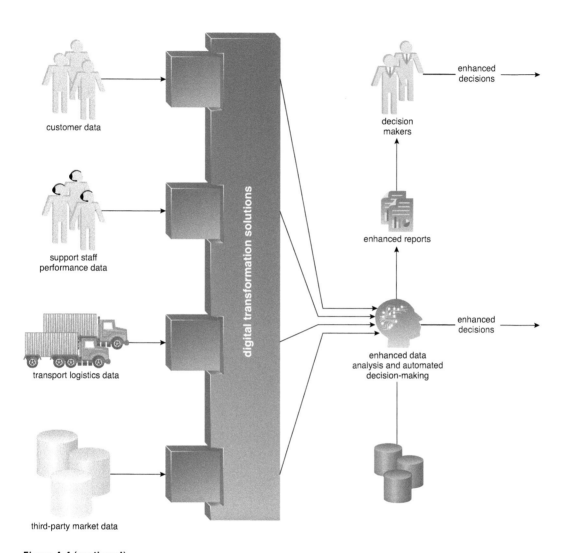

Figure 4.4 (continued)

Improved Organizational Agility

Digital transformation can transform an organization to become more agile in its ability to:

- Adapt to unforeseen business changes, such as new or existing disruptive competitors (that may be introducing new or improved products into a market), internal changes (the resignation of key executives, changes in internal funding, labor unrest), regulatory changes (new taxes, policies and other regulations that affect how a business operates) (Figure 4.6).

- Swiftly introduce new products or services into a market so as to maximize its ability to disrupt an existing marketplace before competitors can adapt and respond.

- Refine and adjust its business processes and models in response to new data intelligence, which the organization will also want to carry out swiftly to maximize potential benefits before competitors can themselves adjust.

This increased level of organizational agility can enable businesses to maneuver in response to planned or unplanned business change, with less impact to its operations and automation solutions.

> **TIP**
> Digital transformation solutions are ideally designed to evolve with the organization's business. This means that as the business changes, the underlying automation solutions are updated to enable those changes, preferably with minimal application development impact. To support this, a DevOps approach can be considered, along with technology architecture models that advocate broad standardization, such as SOA.

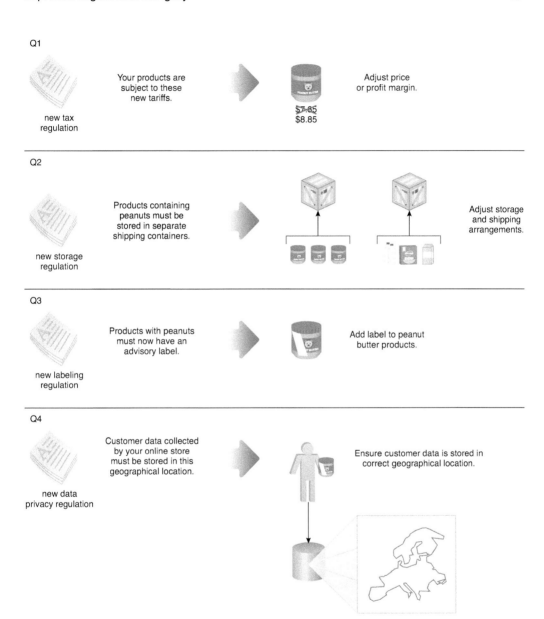

Figure 4.6

Over the course of a year, a business selling food products is required to adapt to a series of regulatory changes that impact some of its products. The improved alignment of its underlying automation systems allows the organization to more efficiently adjust its operations to accommodate such unforeseen changes.

Improved Ability to Attain Market Growth

Digital transformation platforms enable an organization to make significant enhancements in how its business currently operates and, often more importantly, to introduce new products and services to disrupt existing markets in pursuit of growth.

This can lead to several avenues for increasing market share and revenue, such as:

- being able to reach a wider range of customers by moving more products and services online

- being able to reach new customers by adding new products and services to their offerings

- being able to increase the frequency of (existing and new) customers returning by improving customer experience

Furthermore, the technologies associated with digital transformation provide many opportunities for underlying automation solutions to become highly optimized, such as:

- optimizing business workflows by improving the quality of automation technology

- optimizing organization-wide workflows by introducing new automation technology in support of cross-departmental collaboration

- carrying out tasks faster and with less overhead by replacing manual labor with automation logic

- carrying out decisions in realtime and with less expense by replacing human decision makers with automated decision logic

- continually improving and refining business operations in response to new digital data intelligence that is collected, analyzed and fed into decision-making responsibilities carried out by humans and machines

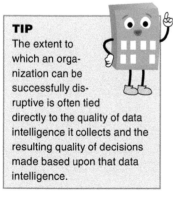

TIP
The extent to which an organization can be successfully disruptive is often tied directly to the quality of data intelligence it collects and the resulting quality of decisions made based upon that data intelligence.

By repeatedly building upon these enhancements, organizations can continue to optimize their operations while continuing to increase the scope and revenue potential of their businesses (Figure 4.7).

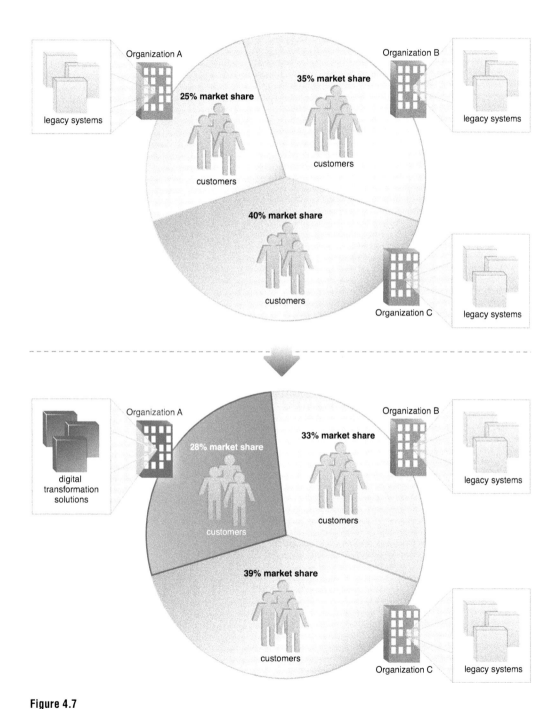

Figure 4.7
Organization A aims to increase its market share by 3% as a result of a successful digital transformation whereby it plans to improve existing services and products and introduce new services and products into the marketplace.

Chapter 5

Common Risks and Challenges (What Are the Pitfalls?)

Poor Data Quality and Data Bias

Increased Quantity of Vulnerable Digital Data

Resistance to Digital Culture

Risk of Over-Automation

Difficult to Govern

Know the hurdles to know how to best get past them!

It's always better to be ready for a pitfall so that instead of risking a fall into a pit, you turn it into a hurdle that you can prepare yourself to jump over.

This chapter covers challenges that can significantly sidetrack or even derail a digital transformation effort. Let's start getting ready for those hurdles.

Due to the potential scope of a digital transformation, the risks and challenges associated with this type of effort are magnified and need to be carefully assessed to avoid transforming an organization in the wrong direction.

This chapter covers the following common risks and challenges associated with carrying out digital transformation:

- Poor Data Quality and Data Bias

- Increased Quantity of Vulnerable Digital Data

- Resistance to Digital Culture

- Risk of Over-Automation

- Difficult to Govern

Poor Data Quality and Data Bias

As previously explained, digital transformation solutions are heavily data-driven. The data intelligence utilized and produced by these solutions ends up influencing or even determining the outcome of key business decisions. The quality and success of the decision-making is directly proportional to the quality of the data intelligence upon which the decisions are based.

> **CAUTION**
> An added danger is the fact that it can sometimes take a long time before inaccurate or biased data results are discovered. By that time, the organization may have already made a series of poor decisions based on flawed data intelligence.

A constant, overarching concern associated with digital transformation is the completeness, accuracy and orientation of the data used to produce data intelligence. If the quality of the data is poor or sub-par, it can lead to misleading analysis results or missed opportunities to discover new insights (Figure 5.1). Another related concern is data bias, whereby some factors within the data are more heavily weighted than others, leading to skewed results and analytical errors.

This challenge is mitigated by ensuring that data scientists working with the data have the necessary skills and proficiency to identify and filter out "bad" data. Sound quality assurance practices are also necessary.

Increased Quantity of Vulnerable Digital Data

A digital transformation initiative will introduce higher volumes of business data and will often encourage a greater digital presence online. This can expose significantly greater amounts of an organization's business data to the outside world. This can, consequently, increase the risks that such data is accessed and manipulated by unauthorized parties (Figure 5.2).

Cybersecurity technologies and practices provide increased protection for organizations with a large online presence. Some cybersecurity systems utilize data science technologies to more effectively profile attackers and counter malicious activity.

> **NOTE**
> Blockchain technology can be also utilized to improve the security and immutability of storage for select data. However, the bulk of digital data will likely continue to remain stored in standard repositories that will need to be carefully secured.

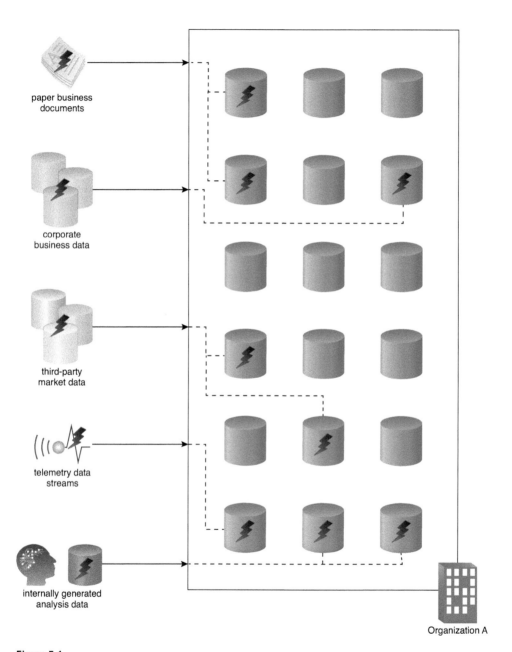

paper business
documents

corporate
business data

third-party
market data

telemetry data
streams

internally generated
analysis data

Organization A

Figure 5.1

Low-quality data and data bias can creep into almost any type of data collected by an organization. If undetected, it can make
its way into a range of internal corporate repositories where it can influence data intelligence used as input for both manual
and automated decision-making.

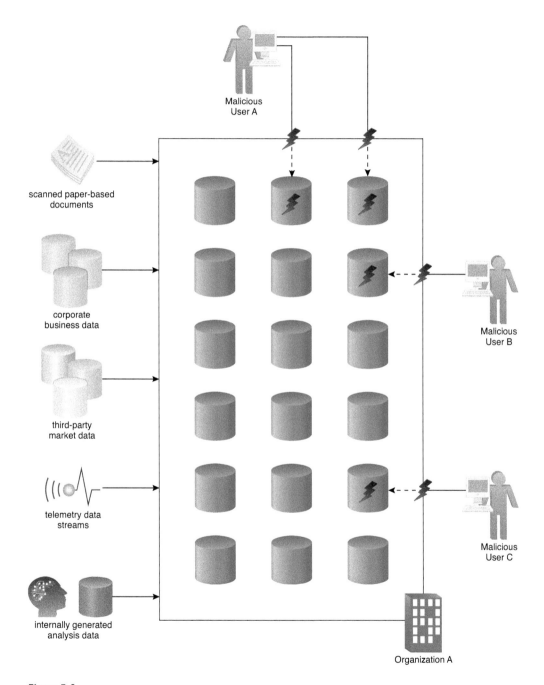

Figure 5.2
The increasing quantity of data flowing into an organization can correspondingly increase the opportunities for malicious users to gain unauthorized access.

Resistance to Digital Culture

A digital transformation aims to change and improve an organization as a whole. This can include transforming:

- the nature and scope of an organization's business

- how humans work and what tasks they are assigned

- how organizations carry out their day-to-day operations

- the extent to which automation becomes part of an organization's operations

Such an initiative will naturally also transform the overall culture of an organization.

For example:

- groups and departments that previously did not need to communicate often may now need to collaborate on a regular basis

- departments that had full authority over their respective business domains may now lose or need to share that authority

- employees that previously performed manual tasks may be replaced with new automation technology capable of performing those tasks faster and at a lower cost (Figure 5.3)

These are just some of the scenarios that can lead an organization's workforce to resist the introduction of digital transformation.

Figure 5.3
Various staff may initially resist digital transformation. It is common for there to be concerns about job loss and a move toward a culture that can appear to be "colder" and more calculating when it comes to decision-making.

Quality leadership can provide pre-emptive efforts, along with new organizational models, to help mitigate resistance and help foster greater support for digital transformation. Management can ensure that the organization is transformed with the most positive outcomes, for both the business and the human workers.

For example, many organizations do not simply lay off employees whose prior contributions are superseded by new automation; they invest in the retraining and reallocation of those employees to further contribute to the organization at a greater and more meaningful capacity.

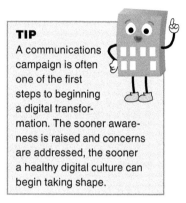

TIP
A communications campaign is often one of the first steps to beginning a digital transformation. The sooner awareness is raised and concerns are addressed, the sooner a healthy digital culture can begin taking shape.

Risk of Over-Automation

The digital transformation market offers a variety of new opportunities to introduce automation into business operations. In many cases, the benefits are clear and tangible, especially in relation to cost savings and improved time-to-value benefits. However, there are often reasons as to why some automation options may simply not be suitable, either now or in the future.

For example:

- Many of the new automation opportunities are driven by the availability of analytical data that is used to feed into new solution logic. The quality or maturity of the data itself may not yet be sufficient to warrant replacing manual tasks with automation (Figure 5.4). This is a case where the automation of certain tasks may need to be delayed until the necessary input data is assessed and considered ready.

- The organization itself may not have reached a sufficient level of maturity to establish some forms of automation on a broader scale. Perhaps the necessary levels of collaboration have not yet been achieved to create the required level of organizational alignment, or perhaps there is too much resistance to the "digital culture." Another consideration is the quality of existing business processes. Automating poor business processes does not address their shortcomings and can even reduce the motivation to fix their problems once new automation is in place.

CAUTION
Recovering from an over-automation can be painful, as it may require reversing recent changes to workflow, human worker allocation and digital transformation solution logic. To avoid this, it is best to carefully assess, in advance, each new automation opportunity.

The technology innovations introduced by digital transformation can be powerful and impactful and can change the landscape of an IT enterprise. Their introduction therefore needs to be carefully planned and phased in as part of the greater digital transformation initiative.

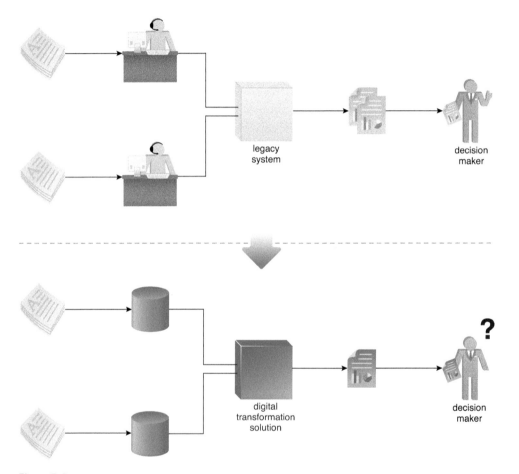

Figure 5.4

A legacy accounting system that previously relied on the manual processing of paper business documents is replaced with a fully automated digital transformation solution. However, the resulting reporting produced is not valuable because the solution was unable to replicate the quality of the human data entry. A better solution may have been to still digitize the paper business documents while retaining the involvement of the human resources.

Difficult to Govern

Governance is a key success factor in many IT initiatives to ensure that the introduction of new and improved technologies achieves an organization's tactical and strategic goals. However, the potential governance scope of a digital transformation effort can be unpredictable and daunting and and will go well beyond IT (Figure 5.5).

Digital transformation can introduce several far-reaching impacts to both business and IT that need to be tracked, assessed and regulated in order for the initiative to proceed and evolve successfully over time.

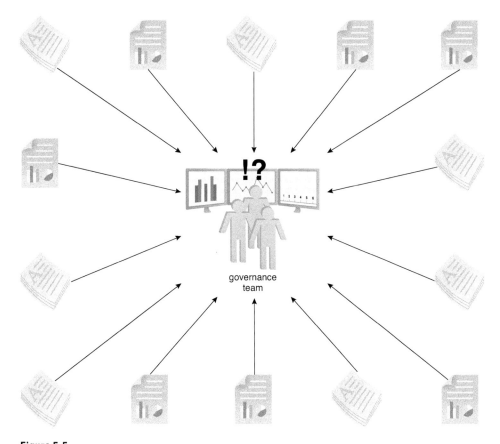

Figure 5.5

A governance group comprised of business and technology professionals is responsible for the governance of an organization's digital transformation. This team may be challenged to stay on top of the many governance processes and precepts that may be established, created and coordinated.

For example:

- The merging of existing business processes and models and the introduction of new products and services (that further introduce new business processes and models) need to be carefully orchestrated and evolved to ensure they fulfill expectations.

- The introduction of new technology platforms can supplant legacy systems entirely, or require new forms of integration with legacy environments.

- The introduction of data-driven technology solutions can change the design and technology architecture of existing automation solutions that perform common automated tasks.

- The automation of tasks that were previously performed manually can increase the overall scope and responsibility of IT departments.

- The new forms of cross-silo collaborations that may be required can lead to different ways of budgeting and staffing projects, as well as new assessment criteria and processes.

A governance team comprised of both business and IT professionals needs to be given the responsibility of overseeing and regulating a digital transformation initiative. This team may require significant resources and training to be fully prepared to govern different life cycle stages of many inter-related projects.

TIP
A digital transformation governance framework will often introduce precepts and processes that formalize how different parts of the initiative need to be carried out and how the digital transformation environment itself needs to be maintained.

Chapter 6

Realizing Customer-Centricity

Customers are our best assets!

Instead of viewing customers solely as a source of revenue and as a necessity to operating a business, digital transformation advocates a mindset whereby customers are genuine assets that can provide long-term value as sources of revenue and data. Let's have a look at what it means to be customer-centric.

Many organizations have traditionally focused on the delivery of products *to* customers instead of establishing a focus on the customers themselves. Digital transformation advocates a foundational shift in an organization's business models to transform away from product-orientation (transaction-based customer interactions) and to transform toward customer-orientation (relationship-based customer engagement).

What Is a Product?

A *product* is something that is produced, most commonly with the intention of selling it for revenue or providing it in exchange for something else of value. A product can be a physical item or it can be non-physical, such as the delivery of a service. Examples of physical products include cars, toys, machine parts and computers. Examples of service products include accounting services, delivery services, cleaning services and consulting services.

The purchase of a physical product typically requires a transaction that results in the transfer of ownership of the product from the seller to the buyer. The purchase of a (non-physical) service product will typically involve a transaction for the delivery of the service. Such a transaction does not normally result in the transfer of ownership of the product. And, of course, some transactions may involve the sale of a combination of physical and service products.

Products are typically associated with items purchased from private, for-profit organizations. However, other types of organizations can also offer products. For example, public sector organizations, such as government departments, offer a range of services. These services may not be directly for sale (such as services offered by for-profit organizations) but they are offered to and consumed by customers and often involve the payment of fees.

A common characteristic of physical products and service products is that they both generally have tangible value to the seller and buyer (or customer).

What Is a Customer?

A *customer* is an individual or an organization that purchases or acquires products. Private sector businesses generally exist to serve customers and generate revenue from customer interactions. Public sector organizations often have the responsibility to offer services of value to a public community, generally with the understanding that these organizations exist as a result of the taxes paid by the public community they serve.

Individuals and organizations are not solely customers. Being a customer is a role that is carried out when they order and acquire products. While an organization may be a customer when it acquires products from one supplier, the organization itself may then assume the role of supplier when it sells its own to another organization (which then assumes the role of customer), as illustrated in Figure 6.1.

NOTE
The customer-orientation emphasis of digital transformation does not only apply to active customers that are purchasing or acquiring products. It applies equally to *potential* customers, which may be individuals or organizations that have not yet become customers but have been identified as customer candidates.

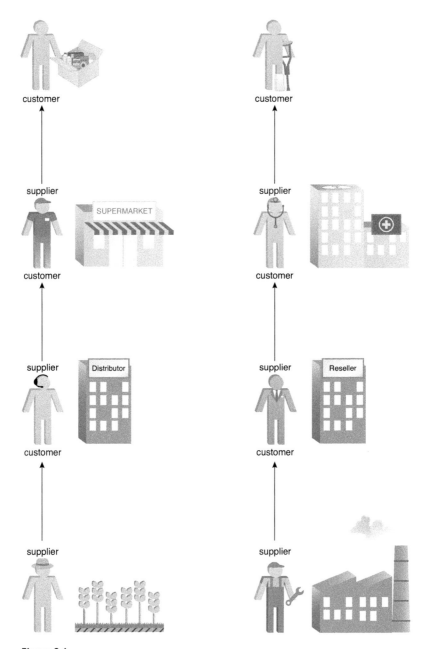

Figure 6.1
Different supply chains involving different parties, several of which assume both customer and supplier roles.

Product-Centric vs. Customer-Centric Relationships

Almost any type of organization is required to interact with customers. Traditionally, the emphasis of organizations has been primarily on the quality of the product it offers. The assumption here is that the greater the value (or perceived value) of a product, the greater the satisfaction of the customer acquiring the product. This is a product-centric organizational model.

In a product-centric organization the product is the primary business entity around which many parts of the organization are built and structured. When an organization has several products, there has been a common tendency to build a separate organizational domain around each product. This can lead to silo-based organizational structures that become fragmented over time as each silo carries on its own lifecycle and direction.

A customer-centric organization positions the customer as the primary business entity and then positions other parts of the organization (including relevant products and value-add services) with the goal of maximizing successful interactions and transactions with its customers. To achieve this goal, many of the previously silo-based organizational departments are required to collaborate. The result is a broad organizational transformation that goes well beyond being "extra nice" to customers and extends into how technology is utilized to build customer-centric automation solutions.

A classic example is a product-centric bank that has organizational silos for its current product portfolio, which may include savings accounts, mortgages, insurance and investments. This product-centric business model leads to customers having to interact individually with the bank when inquiring about or acquiring each product. A customer acquiring all four products may, resultantly, end up having to create and manage four separate customer accounts. A subsequent maintenance task, such as updating an address or phone number, may have to be repeated four times.

This approach predictably leads to a sub-optimal customer experience. In this example, customers may have felt as though they purchased four products from four different banks. This approach is also not ideal for the organization, as it ends up with redundant and out-of-synch customer data and often an inability to gain genuine data analysis insights into customer trends and statistics.

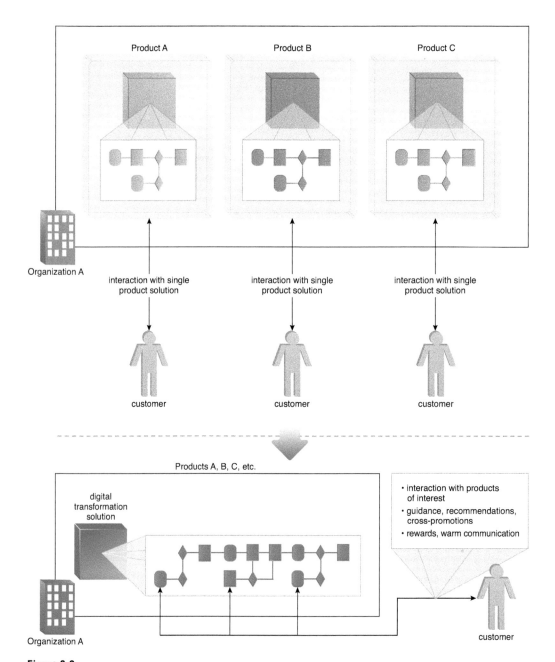

Figure 6.2

A product-centric organization (top) has organizational silos that have established a dedicated business process for each product. As a result, the customer must interact with each product solution individually. After the organization becomes customer-centric (bottom), the silos are removed and the business processes consolidated to provide a single interaction experience during which the customer can learn about and purchase any products of interest, and during which the customer is motivated to return on a regular basis.

When fostering relationship-centric customer engagements, the customer experience does not end after the purchase of a new product. Instead, that is often the starting point of what the organization hopes is to become a genuine relationship with the customer and a relationship that is not limited to the customer's interest in a given product (Figure 6.2). In fact, an organization may even pursue a long-term relationship with a customer who has not even purchased a product, but who perhaps fits the profile of a customer type that is viewed as a potential corporate asset.

Transaction-Value vs. Relationship-Value Actions

During a transformation toward a customer-centric business model, the individual interactions that comprise business processes, workflows and interaction scenarios are often carefully studied and classified as follows:

- *Transaction-Value Action* – A short-term result from an interaction with a "one-off" activity that is not primarily geared toward making the customer return classifies the interaction as a transaction-value action. For example, the payment step in a product purchase scenario can be considered a transaction-value step that is essentially a one-off action that does not lead to further activities from the customer to increase their value to the organization.

- *Relationship-Value Action* – A long-tern result from an interaction that is intentionally geared toward making the customer return classifies the interaction as being a relationship-value action. For example, the aforementioned payment step could be remodeled as a relationship-value activity by awarding the customer with credit or points that the customer can apply toward a future purchase. Each purchase motivates the customer to return again, thereby fostering a relationship.

These examples are over-simplified. For most business processes, the transitioning of interactions from transaction-value to relationship-value can involve significant analysis and business modeling efforts. In many cases, this will require different departments and project teams to collaborate in new ways (as previously explained in the *Enhanced Business Alignment* section in Chapter 4).

Note also that not all customer interactions need to be relationship-value based. There may be several steps and actions within a given scenario that do not warrant or cannot support a transformation toward relationship-value. What is of primary importance is that the overall business process is sufficiently improved to have shifted from being product-centric to customer-centric in support of the organization's digital transformation goals (Figure 6.3).

Figure 6.3

An online order business process with transaction-value steps simply receives information from the customer and concludes the transaction (top). The same online order business process is remodeled so that Steps 1 and 3 become relationship-value actions aimed to increase customer satisfaction and that encourage the customer to return (bottom).

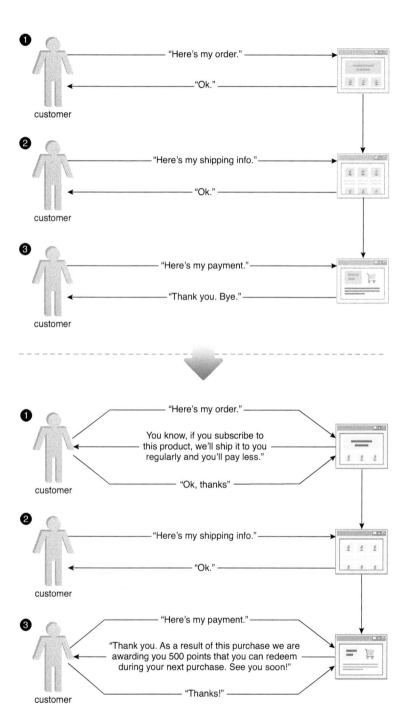

Customer-Facing vs. Customer-Oriented Actions

When breaking down business processes associated with customer activity, there is a need to separate actions into two further categories:

- *Customer-Facing Actions* – An action or activity initiated by or resulting from direct customer interaction is a customer-facing action. An example is when a customer interacts with an online store to place an order.

- *Customer-Oriented Actions* – An action or activity associated with assisting a customer or supporting a customer relationship but that does not involve direct interaction with the customer is considered a customer-oriented action. An example is when a customer orders a product that is not in stock, and behind-the-scenes steps are taken to process a backorder for the customer. Another example is ensuring that solutions used by customers remain consistently operational so that the customer does not have to experience unexpected outages.

When migrating to a customer-centric business model, an effort is made to transition transaction-value actions that are both customer-facing and customer-oriented to becoming relationship-value actions, wherever applicable (Figure 6.4).

Relationship Value and Warmth

Warmth represents the extent of friendliness and accommodation a solution and/or human workers can exhibit and express to the customer. When designing new solutions or transforming the transaction-value steps of existing solutions to relationship-value steps, there is often a need to carefully assess and determine the appropriate level of warmth to be provided in each relationship-value action. This is especially the case with customer-facing actions where the level of warmth is explicitly expressed to customers.

There are different ways in which warmth can be provided. Some common examples include:

Warmth in Communication

The tone and language of communication used with customers is often, by default, formal, polite and concise. This is because customer communication has traditionally been geared toward professionalism and efficiency, rather than relationship-building.

TIP
Warmth in communication. That's what I'm here for!

customer-facing actions   customer-oriented actions

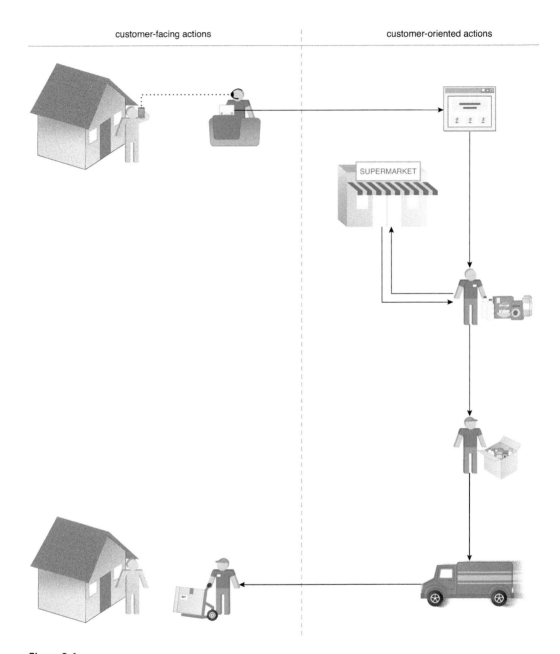

Figure 6.4
When a customer places an order for grocery items to be home-delivered, a series of steps is triggered, only the first and last of which are actually customer facing.

When determining the *communicative warmth* of a digital transformation solution, a number of factors can come into play:

- The tone of communication may be set or altered, which can affect the language and illustration used in both relationship-value steps as well as transaction-value steps. For example, the customer-facing web pages for an online store may be redesigned to provide statements directed at customers using more casual, friendly or encouraging wording expressed by likeable cartoon characters (Figure 6.5).

- Human phone and chat operators may be retrained to interact with customers in a more friendly manner. This may require learning new scripts as well as developing some new social skills to strike up casual conversation during waiting times.

- Other customer-facing employees, such as customer service and delivery personnel, may be trained to improve their social skills so as to treat customers with an increased sense of courtesy and genuine interest.

- The branding of an organization itself may be augmented to appear less cold and corporate. Instead, the branding may be designed to be more personable and relatable to the target customer-base.

Introducing these types of "warmth" alone will likely not turn a given transaction-value action into a relationship-value action. However, applying a level of warmth, where appropriate, does increase the overall customer-centricity of a solution.

Figure 6.5

An online application is updated to change the tone and language of communication, further supplemented with warm graphics.

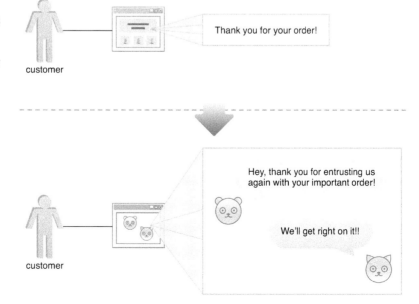

Warmth in Proactive Accommodation

There are sometimes opportunities to introduce *proactive warmth* in customer-facing and customer-oriented actions. Sometimes, these actions are carried out in support of a customer's well-being. Other times, these types of actions are carried out due to a necessity to maintain a guarantee to a customer when unforeseen problems arise. Either way, this type of warmth often requires that the solution or the human worker be creative in how they are proactive.

For example:

- A customer places an order from an online vendor and is promised a 3-day shipping period. However, there is an unavoidable one-day delay in retrieving the product ordered and it cannot be provided to the courier in time for the 3-day shipping service to deliver it at the originally promised delivery date. Instead of notifying the customer that the shipment will be late, the solution or a back-end worker proactively decides to use a 2-day shipping method. Even though this action will end up costing the vendor more, resulting in less or no revenue from the sale, keeping its original shipping guarantee to the customer is considered a priority in order to maintain a long-lasting customer relationship.

> **TIP**
> For many organizations, customer-oriented proactive accommodation is critical to developing long-term customer relationships. The longer a customer interacts with a business without experiencing problems, the greater the reliance and trust the customer develops over time—and —the lower the chance the customer will look elsewhere when a problem does occur.

- A customer places an order from an online vendor for a quantity of six food items. After accepting the order, the vendor realizes that only four of these items are in stock. Instead of issuing a partial refund and shipping a partial order, the vendor replaces the two missing food items with two other, comparable food items. The payment is still partially refunded, but the customer is given complimentary product as a means of mitigating the inconvenience of not receiving exactly what they ordered.

In the former example, the warmth is "transparent" in that the vendor did not add any noticeable warmth to its customer interaction, but instead proactively avoided a situation that could have led to the customer being disappointed and losing confidence.

In the latter example, the warmth is evident to the customer. The vendor also attempts to avoid disappointing the customer but does so by "rewarding" the customer with a gift to offset any negative feelings about the shipment.

In both cases, these extra steps taken by the vendor can be classified as relationship-value actions, as they incur extra effort and expense in support of improving customer-centricity and fostering long-term customer relationships. Therefore, some organizations may utilize their available "customer data intelligence" to analyze and assess customers on a case-by-case basis to determine whether this extra effort and expense are warranted (Figure 6.6). This type of customer profiling is further explored in the upcoming *Customer Data Intelligence* section.

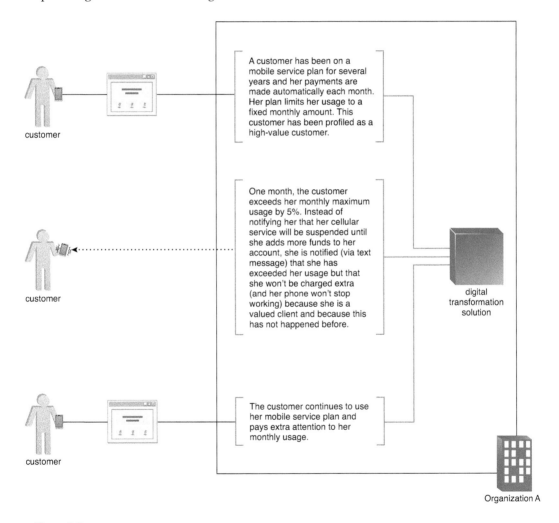

Figure 6.6

A mobile phone company incurs the extra expense of a customer's excess phone usage so as to maintain a positive relationship with what has been profiled as a valuable customer.

Warmth in Customer Rewards

Organizations can increase the *rewardful warmth* of customer interactions by awarding gifts and other types of rewards in recognition of customer value or loyalty. A classic example of this is the reward points system often used with online stores, whereby the customer receives points subsequent to each purchase that can be later redeemed for monetary value. This simple and proven system is effective in encouraging repeat business, but can also become a predictable part of transactions, to the extent that it is not genuinely "warm."

Often, the most effective types of rewards are those that are unexpected by the customer. For example, a mobile service company applying a bonus credit to the last bill of the year in recognition of a customer's one-year anniversary. Or, a law firm sending a food basket to a valuable client after successful negotiations. Unexpected and generous gestures such as these are considered relationship-value actions, as they can provoke positive emotions in customers that will be remembered (Figure 6.7).

Figure 6.7

A customer is surprised to discover a valuable gift certificate in a package with the items originally ordered.

"I wasn't expecting this!!"

customer

Warmth in Exceeding Customer Expectations

Some organizations, especially those trying to distinguish themselves in competitive environments, take customer-centricity to greater levels by trying to deliver *exceeding warmth* in going above and beyond customer expectations.

For example, going back to the prior scenario whereby a vendor proactively avoided a late shipment by incurring additional effort and expense, the vendor may conversely ship an order faster than promised so as to impress a customer and make the customer feel valuable and special.

These types of relationship-value actions that exceed customer expectations are often accompanied with warm communication to clearly inform the customer of the extra effort made and to ensure the customer knows that this was performed just for them. This can provoke even stronger positive emotions than receiving periodic rewards, as it can more clearly express a sense of genuine appreciation. The extra effort may also result in concrete value to the customer (such as the value from receiving an ordered item faster without extra cost) (Figure 6.8).

Figure 6.8

A car service garage exceeds a customer's expectations by proactively providing extra complimentary services that are of concrete benefit to the customer.

"I just asked for an oil change."

"We also cleaned, vacuumed and waxed your car because you are important to us!"

customer

TIP
How and to what extent warmth types are applied may also be related to an organization's understanding of a given customer. Some customers may be more or less responsive to different types of warmth. A digital transformation solution can factor that into how it interacts with a customer, based on the insights it collects from the customer's profile (see the upcoming *Customer Data Intelligence* section).

Single vs. Multi vs. Omni-Channel Customer Interactions

Customers are generally able to complete the same task by interacting with an organization in different ways. For example, traditionally, a customer would be able to place an order by calling a store or by visiting the store in person. Each interaction option is referred to as a *channel*.

If the store would not take orders over the phone and would only offer transactions for those visiting the store in person, its ordering business process would be considered *single-channel*, because only one interaction option is offered to the customer. In the aforementioned case where the store also offered phone-in orders, its ordering business process would be considered *multi-channel*.

For most customer interaction scenarios, single-channels are rare and multi-channels are common. For example, a customer can purchase an item from a physical store just as easily as visiting the company's online store. The problem with multi-channel interactions is that the customer experience with each channel is usually completely independent. If a customer visits a store and asks to put a product on back-order, a multi-channel environment would not necessarily carry over that back-order to the customer's online store account.

Let's imagine the customer originally intended to pick up the back-ordered item from the store, but later decided to arrange for the item to be shipped to the customer's home. With a multi-channel ordering process, the customer would need to phone the store to cancel the original back-order and then log onto the online store to place a new back-order for the product to be shipped to the home address.

Digital transformation advocates an *omni-channel* approach, whereby customer interactions across multiple channels are kept in synch. Digital transformation further advocates a *multiexperience* approach whereby customers have a wide range of access methods made available to them.

Examples of the types of channels commonly supported by *multiexperience* environments include:

- web-based online accounts
- phone and virtual communication
- online chats
- email exchanges
- in-person visits
- paper-based letter or document exchanges

Examples of the types of devices commonly supported by *multiexperience* environments include:

- laptops and workstations
- smartphones and tablets
- smart watches and other wearables
- smart TVs
- voice-activated devices

Omni-channel support is a key aspect of customer-centric solution design that provides the following benefits (Figure 6.9):

- Customer satisfaction is increased because customers become aware of the fact that they can switch from one channel to another without having to repeat previous actions. This is especially important with customer interaction scenarios that can take longer periods of time, in which case customers especially appreciate the flexibility of being able to discontinue on one channel and then continue later on another.

- The organization's labor and effort associated with the customer interactions is streamlined because there is less need to accommodate changes, cancellations and redundant process steps across multiple interaction scenarios.

- There are increased opportunities to add relationship-value actions to the overall customer experience because some channel mediums can provide more enhanced customer-centric features than others. For example, a customer that initially visits a store and then switches to an online interaction can now be served online ads, recommendations and rewards that may not be possible during the in-person visit.

Not all customer-related business processes require omni-channel support. Sometimes the nature of the interaction simply does not warrant more than a single channel. For example, an organization may decide to limit its technical support to a single-channel chat window. In other cases, the organization may not be willing to invest in the labor and overhead required to support multiple types of customer processing for the same task.

The latter concern can be sometimes addressed by digital transformation technology innovations that enable the automation of some channel interaction. The usage of back-end data science technologies to automate chat conversations with customers is a common example.

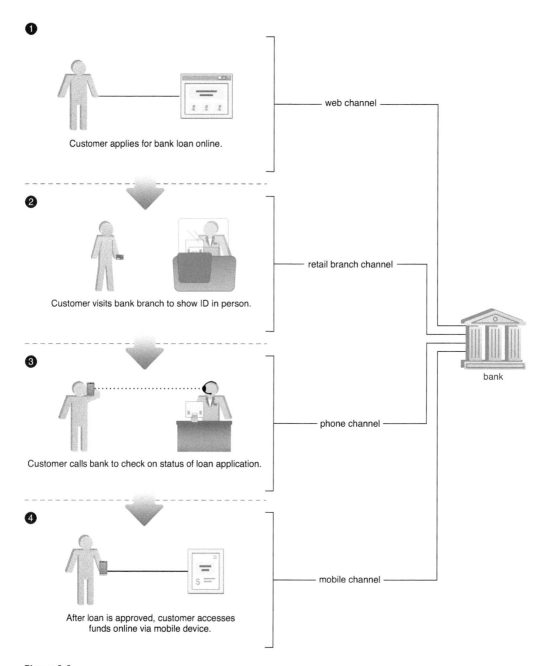

Figure 6.9

A customer interacts with a bank to apply for and eventually collect a loan. Each step involves interaction via a different channel. Because the bank's loan solution is designed to support omni-channel processing, the customer never needs to repeat any part of the interaction.

Customer Journeys

A customer journey is the collection and sequence of steps and actions a customer carries out when interacting with an organization, a product or a service, in order to achieve a goal.

For example:

- A customer that visits an online store may first interact with the store to browse available products. Then, after choosing a product to purchase, the customer interacts with the shopping cart to choose a shipping option, and finally the customer will interact with the store to process the payment for the order. This customer journey was comprised of these interactions with the goal of buying a product. In this case, the customer journey lasted perhaps a few minutes.

- A customer that visits a mobile phone store may first interact with a sales clerk to purchase a phone and may then interact with a phone support employee to choose a phone number and have the phone registered. The customer may further interact with a website to have the phone activated. In this case, the customer journey is based on omni-channel interactions that may last hours or even days.

Customer journeys can vary in length, scope and complexity. A given customer journey typically spans more than one customer interaction. Customer journeys beyond a single transaction are often considered relationship-building customer journeys (Figure 6.10). A primary objective of digital transformation initiatives is to make customer journeys as customer-centric as possible so that the nature of the relationship-building that occurs leads to positive, recurring customer journeys.

TIP
To experience a customer journey with a customer-centric digital transformation solution, have a look at Chapter 12.

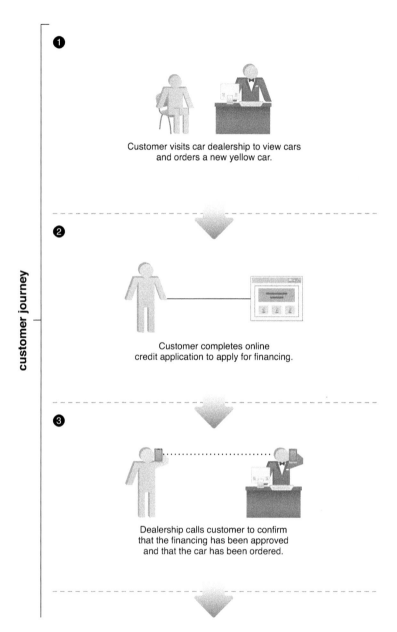

Figure 6.10

A customer journey involving interactions with a car dealership over a period of days in order to purchase a new car.

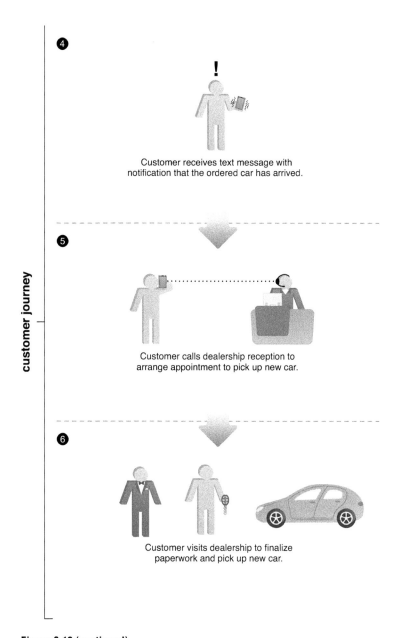

④ Customer receives text message with notification that the ordered car has arrived.

⑤ Customer calls dealership reception to arrange appointment to pick up new car.

⑥ Customer visits dealership to finalize paperwork and pick up new car.

customer journey

Figure 6.10 (continued)

Customer Data Intelligence

A fundamental means by which digital transformation solutions enable and realize customer-centricity is through the extensive collection, processing and analysis of customer-related data.

Examples of the types of customer-related data that can be collected include:

- current contact information
- prior contact information
- geographic location while logging in
- shipping destinations
- shipping speed preferences
- device being used for online access
- interaction patterns
- duration of stay (online session)
- hobbies and interests
- spending behavior
- past purchases
- prior returns
- tone of prior communication (friendly, unfriendly, abusive, etc.)
- relationships and friends with others (customer or non-customer)
- prior reviews and ratings left online

TIP
Different geographical regions have different laws and policies that regulate the use of customer data. For example, regulations can determine which data can be collected, the extent to which permission by the customer is required, where the data can and cannot be stored, for how long it can be retained, for what purpose it can be used, etc.

This type of data is constantly collected in detail and stored in the digital transformation environment (Figure 6.11).

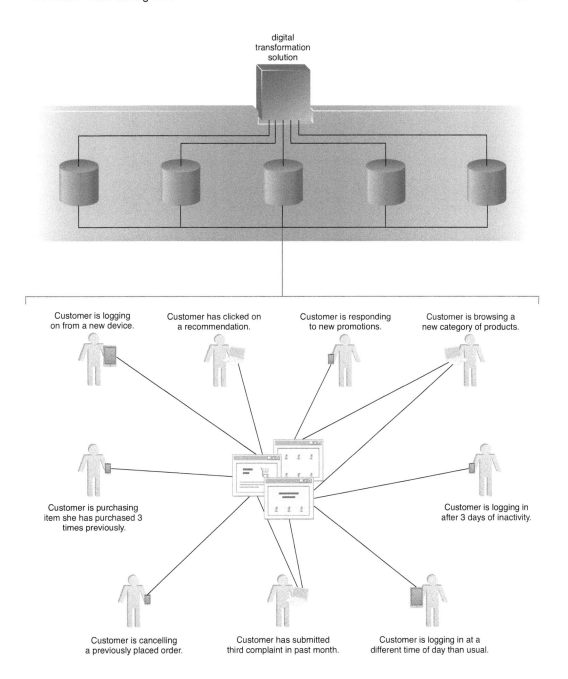

Figure 6.11

A digital transformation solution provides an online application designed to capture and track a range of specific customer-related events and behaviors. Each is stored in a repository where it may be used to create historic customer profiles and also provide input for various analysis and analytics reports to help the organization better identify common customer trends and preferences.

Customer-centric data collected over time helps organizations build profiles of customers by analyzing the accumulated data to derive statistical profiles, such as:

- personality profile (likes, dislikes, preferences, social status, social preferences, etc.)

- session profile (average duration of stay, quantity and types of items viewed, etc.)

- spending profile (average amount spent per visit/week/year, spending habits, etc.)

- relationship profile (responsiveness to promotions, price reductions, recommendations, etc.)

- communication profile (tone and nature of messages, reviews, ratings, etc.)

This type of profile information can be fed into the online solution in realtime to enable it to continually enhance interactions during the next customer visit by customizing its relationship-value actions to the customer profiles. It also enables the solution to take anticipatory actions based on predictions it can derive from analyzing the accumulated customer data.

By combining profile insights with predictions, the solution can determine how to best guide and interact with the customer. For example, it may have logic that determines probabilities and then takes a course of action, as follows:

There is a 78% probability the customer will purchase Products A and B during this visit. Based on the customer's past preferences, there is a 57% probability the customer will be interested in this new Product C. Let's offer the customer a promotion whereby Product C is offered at a 20% discount when purchased together with Products A and B.

Figure 6.12 provides a more detailed interaction scenario.

The previous examples have been focused on cross-promotion and up-selling in relation to retail online sales. It is important to understand that establishing customer-centric experiences and journeys is not always about increasing revenue. For many organizations, such as those in the public sector, the customer is an individual to whom non-revenue generating products or services need to be provided.

In these cases, traditional self-service portals provide relatively simple, transaction-value features that lead to a transaction-centric customer journey. By revisiting the underlying business processes, opportunities to introduce relationship-value steps can be found in an attempt to make the customer journey more customer-centric, as shown in Figure 6.13.

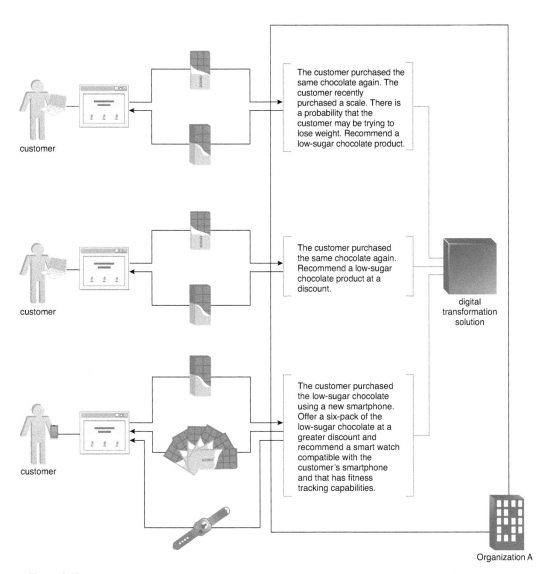

Figure 6.12
As a customer's purchasing profile and behavior changes, the digital transformation solution continuously adapts.

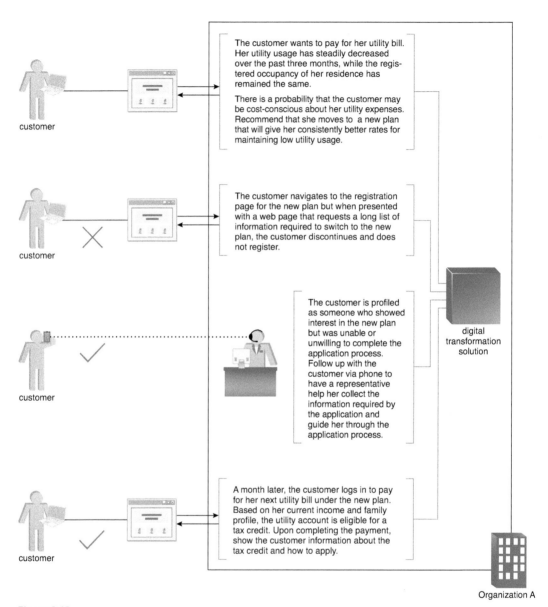

Figure 6.13

A customer is proactively guided to improve their relationship with a utility services organization.

Chapter 7

Data Intelligence Basics

Data Origins (Where Does the Data Come From?)

Common Data Sources (Who Produces the Data?)

Data Collection Methods (How Is the Data Collected?)

Data Utilization Types (How Is the Data Used?)

To get data intelligence, I've got to handle my data intelligently!

Central to planning a digital transformation environment is the data. What relevant data do we already have? What new data do we need? Where will the data come from? What do we do with new data we receive? This chapter establishes some basic concepts to help us get organized so that we can begin juggling our data management responsibilities.

More so than any type of mainstream business applications in the past, what distinguishes digital transformation solutions is the extent to which they are data-driven (Figure 7.1). Many of the critical success factors associated with digital transformation will relate to the quality and quantity of data necessary for the solutions to fulfill their potential and meet expectations.

This chapter explores the following fundamental aspects of acquiring and utilizing data intelligence:

- Data Origins
- Common Data Sources
- Data Collection Methods
- Data Utilization Types

Data Origins (Where Does the Data Come From?)

When assembling a digital transformation environment, it is vital to not only identify the data intelligence requirements, but to also determine which of the data required resides within the organization's ownership and which needs to be externally obtained (Figure 7.2).

In this section, the following data origin types are established:

- Corporate Data
- Third-Party Data

Figure 7.1

Whereas traditional legacy applications often relied on the involvement of one or two databases, digital transformation solutions typically require access to numerous databases.

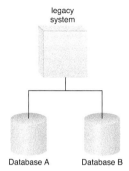

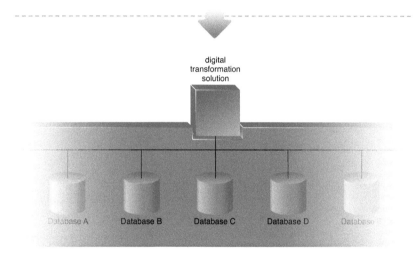

Figure 7.2

As explained shortly, corporate data is internal data owned by an organization, whereas openly available or purchased data is provided by third parties. (Note that subsequent sections that explain data sources and methods also indicate how those topics relate to the corporate and third-party data source types.)

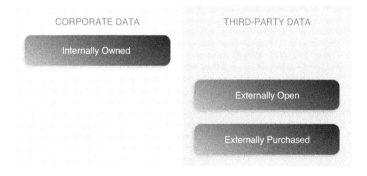

The section concludes by explaining how the acquisition and processing of third-party data can lead to increased corporate data intelligence.

Corporate Data

Corporate data primarily represents data that originates within and is produced by an organization. It is internal data that is owned by the organization and the organization has control over its creation and subsequent governance.

Corporate data is extremely valuable to digital transformation solution processing, as it represents the proprietary "heart" of a business operation. The introduction of data science practices and systems to the processing of corporate data will often reveal new insights and discoveries as to an organization's strengths and weaknesses in different areas (which are typically measured using key performance indicators).

TIP

The idea of having to acquire new data from third-party sources may be new to some organizations. This alone can introduce the need for new employees, IT infrastructure, policies, legal requirements, etc. Furthermore, there needs to be a way to ensure that the quality of any acquired data is acceptable.

Third-Party Data

More so than any traditional automation solution approaches in the past, digital transformation solutions commonly have a reliance on large quantities of data from both internal and external sources. The need to supplement existing corporate data produced and owned by the organization with data from the outside world relates to fundamental goals associated with improving customer relations beyond traditional boundaries and with improving the organization's status and growth within its business community, beyond its traditional standing.

For an organization to exceed its traditional performance levels, it will almost always require insights from intelligence from the outside world. Such intelligence is provided by third-party data providers.

Creating New Corporate Data Intelligence

As already explained, data from outside providers can be acquired, often by being purchased. Although this data is technically then "owned" by the acquiring organization, it is not classified as corporate data, as the origin of the data was not the organization itself.

However, the on-going incorporation of "fresh" outside data into internal digital transformation solution environments will naturally produce quantities of new internally produced data intelligence that can be legitimately considered new corporate data.

Common Data Sources (Who Produces the Data?)

Regardless of the overarching data origin, it is important to understand how and from where data relevant to digital transformation is produced. The following common data sources (Figures 7.3 and 7.4):

- Operations Data
- Customer Data
- Social Media Data
- Public Sector Data
- Private Sector Data

Other data sources exist and may very well be important to some organizations.

NOTE

Common methods for how an organization receives data from these data sources (such as File Push, File Pull, API Push, API Pull and Data Streaming) are covered in the *Data Ingress Basics* section in Chapter 9.

Figure 7.3

While corporate customer data typically originates internally, external customer data is also sought out by organizations to better understand and analyze the marketplace or community beyond the organization's traditional boundaries. While the other types of third-party data can originate as corporate data (depending on the nature of the organization), they are most commonly obtained from third-party data providers.

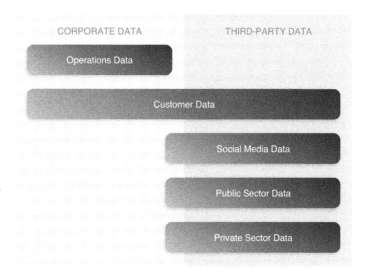

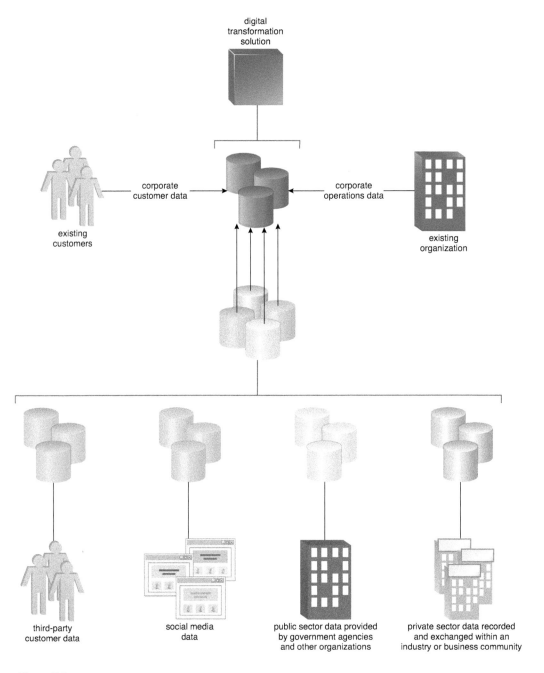

Figure 7.4

A view of common data sources that can provide input for the digital transformation solution.

Operations Data

This is the most internally-focused data source in that it represents data pertaining to how the organization itself operates.

Operations data can include:

- human resources and employee assessment data
- departmental and project performance data
- budgets and other financial data
- sales statistics and quota-related data
- product manufacturing and sales data
- telemetry data from remote sensors

While much of the data relevant to digital transformation solutions is external in nature, operations data is often a vital form of input that enables solutions to adapt to change, scale to usage demands and fulfill customer expectations.

Customer Data

As explained previously in the *Customer Data Intelligence* section in Chapter 6, detailed customer-related activity and profile data can provide extremely valuable insights for assessing, improving and establishing new forms of customer-centric solutions.

Social Media Data

Social media data is contributed voluntarily and spontaneously by individual users and businesses via social media sites and platforms. Social media corporations often have the permission to monetize the data their platforms collect and publish, which can classify them as third-party data providers. Other third-party vendors and firms may have the ability to harvest certain types of social media data and further process it to produce analytics, statistics, trend information and other types of market or community intelligence.

Organizations can use social media data (or data intelligence derived from it) to gain significant and comprehensive insights, such as:

- the preferences, dislikes and interests of social media users that fit the profiles of potential customers

- how other organizations and possible competitors are communicating and relating to social media users

- how advertising on certain social media sites may or may not be effective in growing the organization's business

Social media data that is processed and filtered to provide a collection of data intelligence relevant to an organization's digital solution can be extremely valuable for strategic planning and decision-making purposes.

Public Sector Data

Various government organizations and departments publish data under open licenses that allows it to be freely consumed. Sometimes public sector data needs to be obtained at a cost.

Governments publish various types of historical and regional data, including:

- social, population and habitation data

- infrastructure statistics and planned infrastructure improvements

- traffic, pollution and noise quality data

- electoral data

- budgets and other financial data

- travel advisories

- geospatial data and satellite imagery

- energy consumption statistics

- healthcare data

- vegetation, water quality, environmental data

- regulations, policies and laws

- educational and academic statistics

This type of data is published for various reasons, such as to:

- provide transparency to the population

- promote a government's achievements

- encourage greater citizen engagement
- encourage foreign investment and tourism

Several of these reasons are, in fact, motivated by a desire to make a government more customer-centric.

Depending on the nature of an organization's business (and whether the organization itself is part of a public sector), data published by governments can be used as input to further enhance and shape new corporate data intelligence.

Private Sector Data

Private businesses and organizations that are part of business communities can publish data relevant to their industry and their role in the greater community. There are numerous types of industries with such communities and associations, such as healthcare, finance, automotive, manufacturing, supply chain, etc. Private sector data may be made available openly or only to those organizations in the respective business community.

> **NOTE**
>
> A private sector community may opt to make shared data accessible via blockchain, as explained Chapter 10.

Data Collection Methods (How Is the Data Collected?)

Digital transformation solutions are capable of collecting and storing a broad range of data. The following are common data collection methods:

- Manual Data Entry
- Automated Data Entry
- Telemetry Data Capture
- Digitization
- Data Ingress

The use of some methods can depend on the data origins.

Manual Data Entry

This data collection method occurs when humans manually enter data into a solution. The data may or may not be provided by humans that belong to the organization. For example, a data entry clerk with the organization may be entering accounting data (Figure 7.5), whereas a user outside of the organization may be entering customer or order data.

Figure 7.5
Manual data entry performed by a human.

Automated Data Entry or Collection

Digital transformation solutions may employ the use of bots to automatically enter or collect data (Figure 7.6). Such bots are software programs capable of entering data rapidly and accurately, collecting new data from multiple sources, and automating other administrative tasks that are commonly performed manually.

Figure 7.6
Automated data entry performed by a bot.

Telemetry Data Capture

Another important method of data collection is the capture of telemetry data, which is data that is recorded at remote locations and then transmitted back to the organization and its digital transformation solution for processing and storage.

These systems are based on the wide-spread deployment of sensors capable of collecting different types of data from different environments and geographical regions. The collected telemetry data is typically streamed into a digital transformation solution on a regular basis, often resulting in large quantities of input data (Figure 7.7).

NOTE
The previous two described data collection methods are related to RPA and IoT technologies covered in Chapter 10.

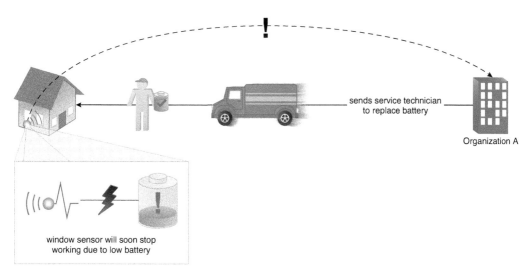

Figure 7.7

A sensor communicates that a battery is near empty. The alarm company receives this telemetry data and sends a service technician to proactively replace the empty battery.

Digitization

Digitization is the process of converting paper documents or analog information into digital data. For most organizations, this process involves scanning large quantities of documents and then subjecting the scanned images to optical character recognition (OCR) systems that are designed to recognize characters in the images and convert them into digital information (Figure 7.8).

Digitization can also be used to convert other types of information into digital data. For example, it can be utilized to convert analog signals, such as temperature measurements, audio recordings, mechanical pressure or weight measurements into forms that can be digitally processed and stored.

TIP
As explained in Chapter 10, parts of the digitization process itself can also be automated.

Regardless of the source of the digitized data, it is often important for the digitization system to supplement it with additional metadata. Adding metadata, such as keywords and categories, establishes the context of the digitized data and ensures that it is correctly recorded and recognized within digital transformation solutions.

Metadata can be added by humans, as part of a manual data entry process, or it can be added automatically by bots that may be further assisted by data science technologies (Figure 7.9).

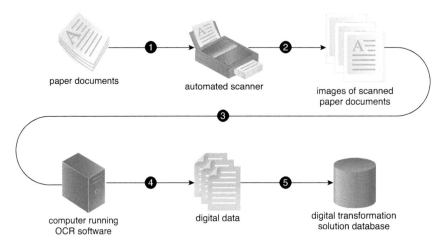

Figure 7.8

Paper documents are scanned (1) to produce electronic images (2). The images are subjected to an OCR program (3) that recognizes the characters in the document to produce machine processable files with digital data (4). The data is stored in a database from where it can be further retrieved, viewed and processed (5).

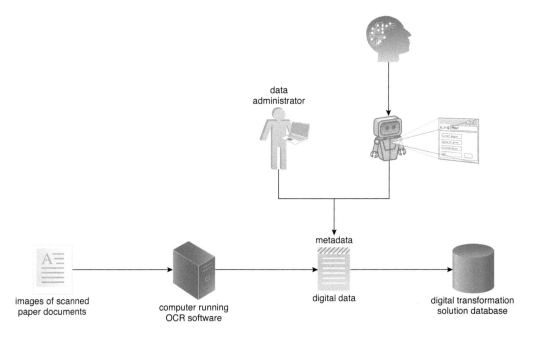

Figure 7.9

Metadata can be added manually by a data administrator that reviews and interprets the digitized data to best determine how it should be tagged with keywords. Alternatively, the digitized data can be analyzed by a data science-powered system that automatically instructs a bot to add the appropriate keywords.

Data Ingress

Digital transformation solutions are typically designed to receive and process entire sets of new data on a regular basis. Data ingress refers to any datasets that are inserted into the solution environment, usually via technical methods, such as batch imports, realtime streaming and programmatically, via APIs.

Of particular relevance is data ingress from data sources that contribute to the accumulation of data intelligence (as further explored in the *Data Ingress Basics* section in Chapter 9).

Data Utilization Types (How Is the Data Used?)

The collection of different types of data via different collection methods is a significant effort and investment that is made to support the ambitious goals and benefits associated with digital transformation. It is therefore vital that there is an understanding of how exactly this data can and will be used by the digital transformation solution (Figure 7.10).

This section explains the following primary utilization types:

- Analysis and Reporting
- Solution Input
- Automated Decision-Making
- Bot-Driven Automation
- Model Training and Retraining
- Historical Record Keeping

Analysis and Reporting

A foundational characteristic of a digital transformation solution is its ability to:

- produce data intelligence in support of guiding the organization, and…
- leverage available data intelligence in support of improving how the organization operates.

As part of the underlying infrastructure of a typical digital transformation lie powerful data processing systems capable of applying sophisticated analysis and analytics practices that produce new data intelligence. These systems rely on contemporary data science technologies. Either via a dashboard or printed reports handed to decision makers, this data intelligence is considered a primary return on investment of digital transformation initiatives.

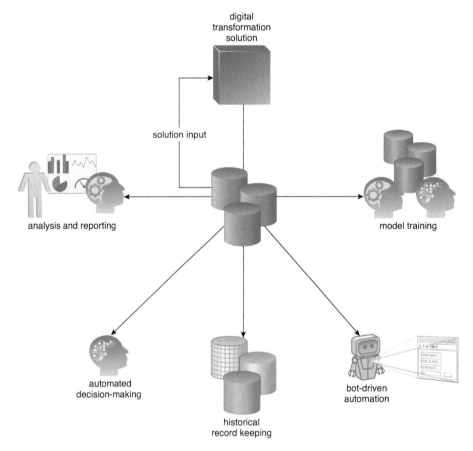

Figure 7.10
Once collected, the vast quantity of diverse data in a digital transformation solution is utilized in many different ways.

Automated Decision-Making

When building a digital transformation solution, there are often several opportunities to allocate decision-making responsibilities to the solution itself. For this to be effective, the automated decision-making logic will be dependent on a constant stream of quality data intelligence.

Data science technologies can be used to create systems with the ability to analyze and assess input data at runtime and to then reason and make decisions based on the analysis and assessment results. The decisions can then be communicated directly to the solution logic to be carried out.

> **NOTE**
>
> The different types of automated decision-making are covered in Chapter 8.

Solution Input

Digital transformation solutions can receive data as input during runtime. Their software programming can be designed to be highly flexible in its ability to receive and act upon a range of input data that can determine how the solution behaves in response to different circumstances.

Bot-Driven Automation

Digital transformation solutions can increase the scope of their automation capabilities by effectively utilizing bots that are capable of receiving input data that determines their actions and behavior.

Data science systems can be used to feed input data to bots, which is the the premise of intelligent automation solutions.

> **NOTE**
>
> Bot-driven automation is further explained in the *Robotic Process Automation (RPA)* section in Chapter 10.

Model Training and Retraining

At the core of self-learning data science systems are *models* that essentially exist as mathematical equations that accept input and produce a result. These models undergo "training" during which they process large quantities of data (Figure 7.11) for the sole purpose of refining and optimizing the mathematical equation so that it continues to evolve to produce increasingly improved results.

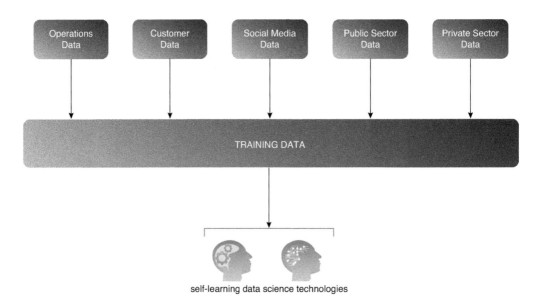

Figure 7.11
Data science systems require training data to enable their models to learn and improve.

Therefore, a large quantity of collected data (especially new data from third-party providers) is often dedicated to training models. This type of data is typically anonymized and historical in nature, enabling the model to learn as much as possible from previous events, records, transactions, etc.

After models are initially trained and then used in production, new training data can be provided to further refine and retrain the models to enable the systems to continuously learn and improve.

Historical Record Keeping

Activity involving human workers, digital transformation solution processing and any of the aforementioned data utilization types will often need to be logged and recorded for future auditing purposes.

NOTE
Often, historical audit data will need to be immutable stored using blockchain technology, as discussed in Chapter 10.

Chapter 8

Intelligent Decision-Making

**To automate,
or not to automate,
that is the question!**

*Data intelligence can help humans make better decisions. The same
systems that help create data intelligence can also be programmed
to act on it. Whether to delegate some decisions to those systems
is a key decision point in and of itself. Let's back up and begin by
comparing the different types of decision-making types. We'll then
move on to take a closer look at automated decision-making.*

Business decisions are made by reviewing some form of input data and then, based on that data (and other relevant data) determining a course of action. Digital transformation solutions aim to improve the intelligence of decision-making, especially in relation to enhancing customer-centricity.

Specifically, digital transformation platforms introduce data processing and analysis technologies that can:

- provide high-quality input data for human decision makers
- provide high-quality input data for automated decision-making systems
- refine input data for automated decision-making systems over time
- learn from the outcome of past automated decisions to continually improve automated decision-making system logic

This chapter covers the following topics:

- Manual Decision-Making
- Conditional Automated Decision-Making
- Intelligent Manual Decision-Making
- Intelligent Automated Decision-Making

The chapter begins by establishing traditional manual and automated decision-making approaches, and then continues by introducing intelligent decision-making approaches that leverage digital transformation technology. The chapter concludes by raising considerations for choosing between manual and automated decision-making.

Manual Decision-Making

Decades ago, all business decisions were made by humans by following a simple process usually comprised of collecting relevant information and then presenting it to a decision maker (Figure 8.1).

Figure 8.1

A human decision maker makes a decision manually, based on report results.

Computer-Assisted Manual Decision-Making

After computers made their debut in office environments, they provided an efficient means of collecting a wide variety of information and compiling it into more meaningful and comprehensive reports. This equipped human decision makers with more information to make improved decisions (Figure 8.2).

Figure 8.2

A human decision maker makes a decision with the help of a computer.

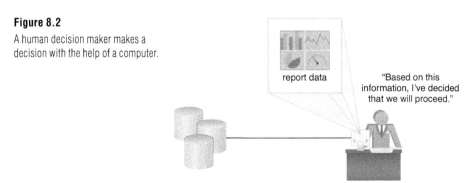

Conditional Automated Decision-Making

Once software programs were being developed to automate different business tasks, there were many opportunities for computer systems to be programmed with logic capable of making simple decisions. This type of pre-defined decision-making logic is called conditional logic (Figure 8.3).

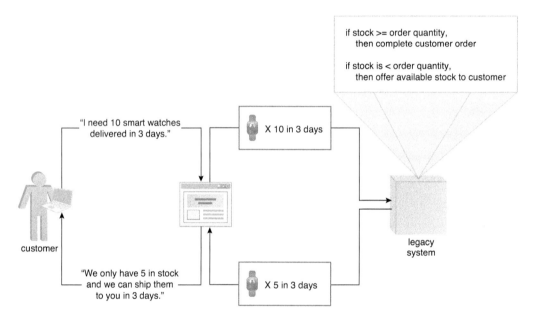

Figure 8.3

A standard legacy system with basic conditional logic that predefines how the system should respond to a situation where the quantity of an ordered item is not in stock.

Conditional logic has remained a core part of computer systems. Over time, the complexity and sophistication of conditional logic has improved. However, while conditional logic can be programmed to accommodate many scenarios, it has many limitations because the usage scenarios need to be predetermined by the system designers in advance.

To improve the outcome of different interaction scenarios and to accommodate unanticipated or more complex scenarios, human decision makers often need to be involved (Figure 8.4).

Intelligent Manual Decision-Making

Contemporary data science systems increased the depth and sophistication of how data could be processed and analyzed. These systems further increased the ability to combine disparate types of data into meaningful data intelligence. These innovations became natural parts of digital transformation environments, and are used to greatly enhance the quality of computer-assisted, manual decision-making (Figure 8.5).

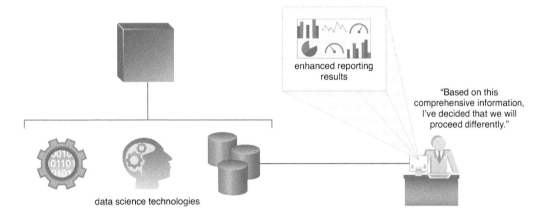

Figure 8.5

A human decision maker makes a more informed decision with the help of a computer that displays reports with deeper and broader analysis results. The presented data may be continually updated to provide on-going decision-making guidance.

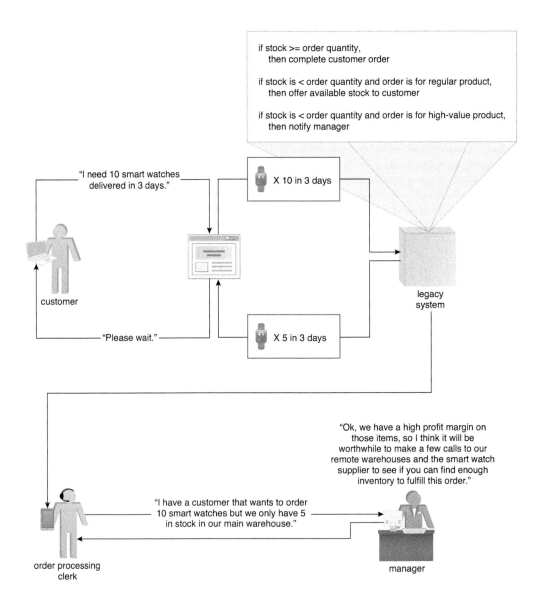

if stock >= order quantity,
    then complete customer order

if stock is < order quantity and order is for regular product,
    then offer available stock to customer

if stock is < order quantity and order is for high-value product,
    then notify manager

"I need 10 smart watches delivered in 3 days."

X 10 in 3 days

customer

"Please wait."

X 5 in 3 days

legacy system

"Ok, we have a high profit margin on those items, so I think it will be worthwhile to make a few calls to our remote warehouses and the smart watch supplier to see if you can find enough inventory to fulfill this order."

"I have a customer that wants to order 10 smart watches but we only have 5 in stock in our main warehouse."

order processing clerk

manager

Figure 8.4

An alternative outcome to the previous customer interaction involves a manager who acts as a decision maker, as well as an order processing clerk that carries out tasks in response to the manager's decisions. Together, the humans improve the outcome by being able to offer the customer an option to fulfil the original order request. However, the time and effort it takes to accomplish this is undesirable and risks losing the customer altogether.

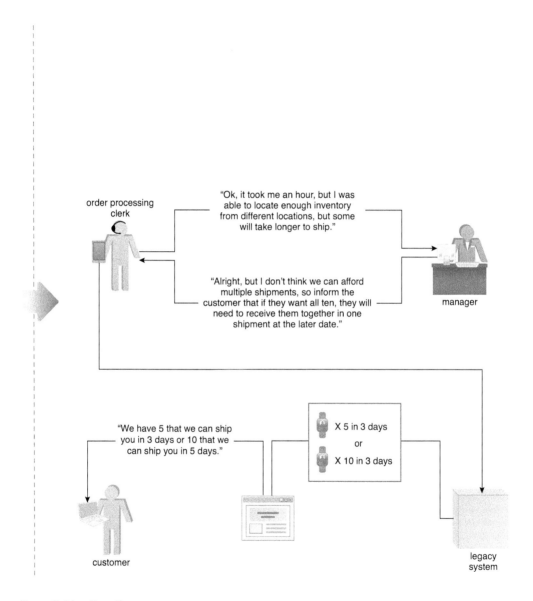

Figure 8.4 (continued)

Intelligent Automated Decision-Making

Digital transformation solutions can incorporate advanced data science technologies capable of efficiently automating both simple and complex decision-making tasks, without the need for human involvement.

When used to carry out automated decision-making, these systems can utilize decisioning (and reasoning) engines capable of analyzing input data, factoring in or cross-referencing the input data with other types of data, and applying additional logic to produce a decision result, often instantly (Figure 8.6).

> **TIP**
> Decision-making, whether it be manual or automated, is classified as "intelligent decision-making" when the decisions are based on the use of data intelligence. Therefore, the quality of the decisions will be tied to the "intelligence quality" of the data.

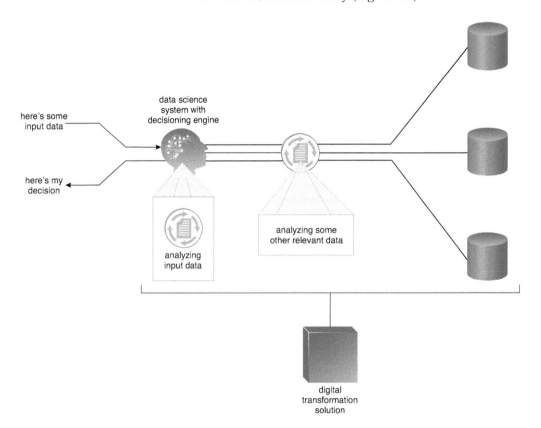

Figure 8.6

A solution with a decisioning engine is capable of rapidly factoring in a range of data to carry out a decision.

Depending on the extent and nature of automation required, there are different ways in which automated decision-making can be part of a solution. The upcoming sections describe the following common types of automated decision-making:

- Direct-Driven Automated Decision-Making

- Periodic Automated Decision-Making

- Realtime Automated Decision-Making

Direct-Driven Automated Decision-Making

When a decision needs to be made ad-hoc, such as when a customer initiates an action that requires that a decision be made, direct-driven decision-making can be utilized. With this approach, the system's decisioning engine is engaged on-demand, usually triggered by user interaction (Figure 8.7).

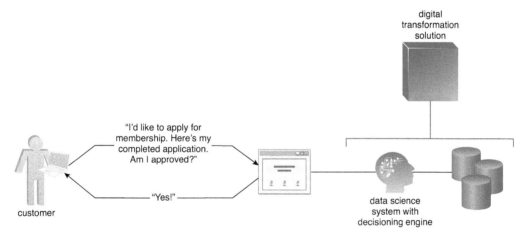

Figure 8.7

The solution assesses the customer's application for membership to a private club. Based on its analysis of relevant data (such as customer profile data, financial history data, etc.), it determines that the customer's request is approved. In this type of scenario, the automated decision-making logic may choose to not make a decision under certain circumstances, such as when insufficient input data is available or when the request is for a certain level of membership that requires further review by a human.

Periodic Automated Decision-Making

Sometimes a solution is required to make decisions based on data that is not always available or sufficiently current. In this case, automated decision-making tasks can be scheduled to occur on a periodic basis (Figure 8.8).

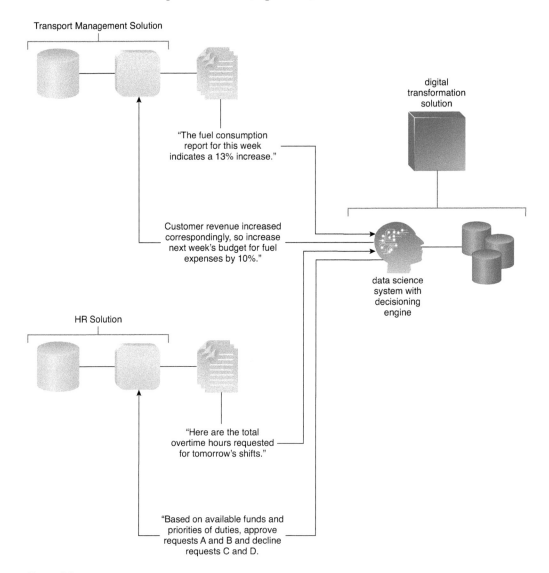

Figure 8.8

The solution is programmed to carry out pre-scheduled decision-making tasks for different automation solutions. It makes decisions based on the data available at the time it carries out its decision-making logic. The solution can further be designed to first ensure a sufficient quantity of relevant data is available before engaging the decisioning engine. If not, it can automatically postpone its decision-making tasks.

Realtime Automated Decision-Making

A data science system and its decisioning engine can be encompassed within a digital transformation solution's overall business automation. This enables the solution logic to request and receive decisions whenever necessary and in realtime (Figure 8.9).

> **CAUTION**
> Realtime auto-
> mated decision-
> making has the
> greatest potential
> to ehance automa-
> tion, but also introduces the greatest risk of damage if poor decisions are being made. This is because the high rate at which these decisions can be carried out does not provide much time to properly assess their outcomes. This form of decision-making in particular should therefore only be used when the quality of the input data is high and the risk of damage is considered reasonable.

Intelligent Manual vs. Intelligent Automated Decision-Making

The choice to defer decision logic to a system, rather than to a human, comes with benefits and risks that need to be carefully considered. A decisioning engine can usually make decisions faster, more decisively and more reliably than a human. However, the decisioning engine will be limited to its technical design, the quality of its programming and the quality of the data it is provided. A human decision maker, on the other hand, may provide a broader range of historical understanding and wisdom, as well as an intangible "gut feeling" that may help the human carry out decisions more successfully.

It therefore comes down to the nature of a given decision that can help determine whether the responsibility of the decision-making should be delegated to a human or a decisioning system.

A number of factors can be taken into account:

- *Quality of Input Data* – The quality of business decisions is directly dependent on the quality of the input data provided upon which decisions are based. If the input data quality is poor or introduces an extent of data bias, then the resulting decisions will have a greater probability of failing.

- *Risk of Decision Outcome* – The risk of damage that may be caused by a poor or incorrect decision is often relational to the extent of confidence data scientists have in the solution's decision-making ability. If confidence is not high, then the solution should not carry out high-risk decisions. Confidence can grow as a solution processes increased volumes of new (training and production) data and demonstrates the ability to self-learn from past failure (Figures 8.10 and 8.11).

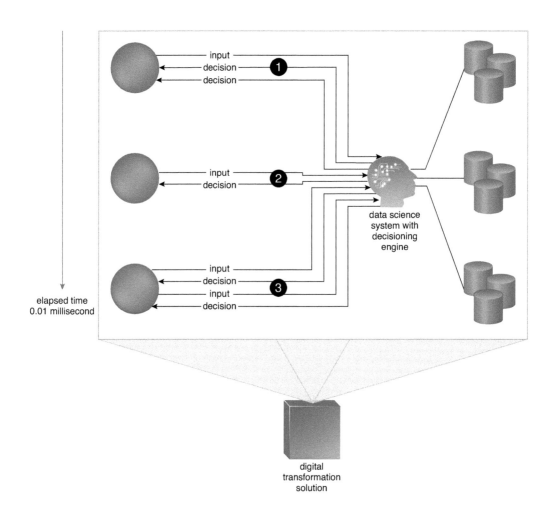

Figure 8.9

The decisioning engine is made part of the internal digital transformation automation logic. Solution logic (contained within "services" depicted as the blue circles) interact with the decision-making logic to request and receive a series runtime decisions (1, 2, 3) in support of the business process logic they are automating.

If it is determined that a solution is making sound decisions on a regular basis, data scientists can choose to allow it to continue or even consider increasing its decision-making responsibilities. If a solution is regularly making poor or incorrect decisions, its decision-making responsibilities can be lessened or removed.

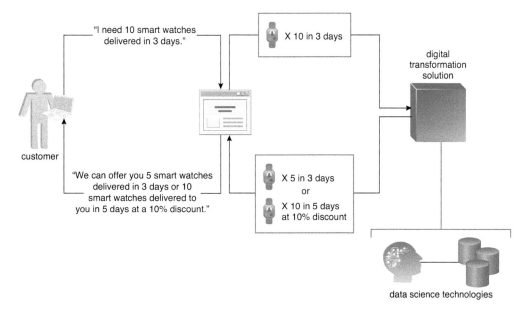

Figure 8.10

This diagram revisits the scenario previously shown in Figure 8.4, only now the solution is given the responsibility of carrying out the decision logic automatically. The solution is able to perform rapid access to information that enables it to determine that, in addition to the 5 smart watches in stock locally, 5 more smart watches are available from other sources. However, it will take longer to provide 10 watches than 5. The solution queries the customer's profile and transaction history and determines that a 10% discount has a 68% probability of enticing the customer to proceed with an order of 10 smart watches.

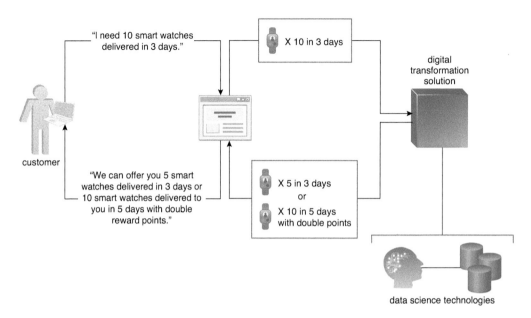

Figure 8.11

In Figure 8.10 the digital transformation solution offered the customer a 10% discount on an order for 10 smart watches. However, data analysts later determine that this was an incorrect decision. Because of inaccurate input data from one of the queried databases, the overall profit margin of the sale had not been fully calculated. As a result, the organization lost money on this transaction. The data analysts take corrective action by updating the input data and subjecting the data science system to further training which enables it to self-learn from its mistake. Under the same circumstance, the solution now offers the customer double reward points (instead of the 10% discount), which it calculates will have a 59% probability of enticing the customer to proceed. Not only will the solution make a better decision in the future due to the improved input data, it has also learned to cross-reference key data to confirm its validity before completing financial calculations.

Part II

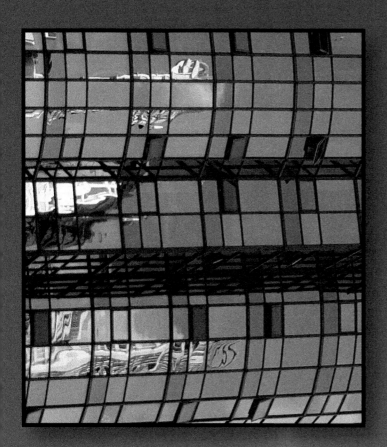

Digital Transformation in Practice

Chapter 9

Understanding Digital Transformation Solutions

Distributed Solution Design Basics

Data Ingress Basics

Common Digital Transformation Technologies

Digital transformation solutions are expected to be powerful, responsive, adaptable to change and highly data-driven. Each solution can be assembled with a different combination of digital transformation technologies. Before we explore those technologies further, let's first cover some of the basic solution components and functions.

A digital transformation initiative will be comprised of many inter-related projects and efforts, ranging from planning, communication and re-education to implementing changes in how staff and departments relate to each other and in how the organization itself operates internally.

A fundamental step to putting digital transformation in practice is to establish the primary technologies responsible for realizing several of the capabilities and strategic benefits covered in the chapters in Part I. This and subsequent chapters in this book are dedicated to introducing these technologies and exploring how they can be combined to support and enable digital transformation solutions.

Distributed Solution Design Basics

A digital transformation solution is an application responsible for automating and/or contributing data intelligence to one or more related business tasks. A major distinguishing characteristic is its need to encompass a broad range of data. This typically results in the requirement for the solution to retain on-going access to a set of data repositories, most commonly databases (Figure 9.1). Each database provide a different type of data relevant to the nature of processing the digital transformation solution needs to carry out.

An organization will typically end up building multiple digital transformation solutions that share IT infrastructure resources, as well as underlying databases (Figure 9.2).

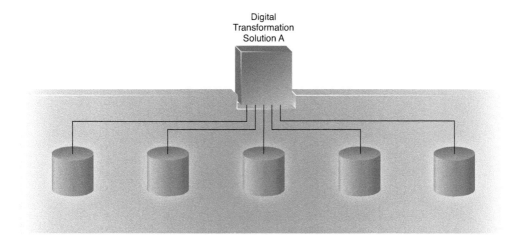

Figure 9.1
A digital transformation solution accessing multiple databases.

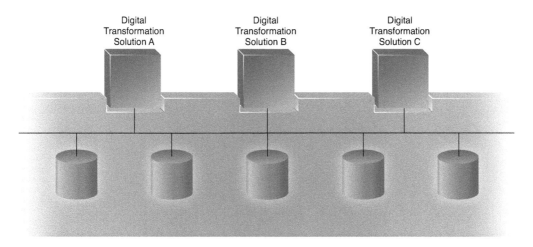

Figure 9.2
Multiple digital transformation solutions co-exist as part of a greater platform. Although individual solutions will typically require some dedicated databases, solutions will often also share access to common databases.

Each digital transformation solution is usually designed as a distributed application, whereby its solution logic is spread across a series of software programs most commonly built as *services* (Figure 9.3).

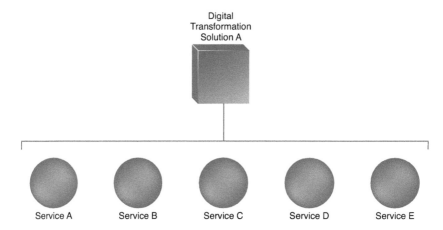

Figure 9.3

The application logic in a given digital transformation solution can be distributed across a number of individual software programs called services.

Services establish the logic layer of a digital transformation solution, whereas databases establish the data layer (Figure 9.4).

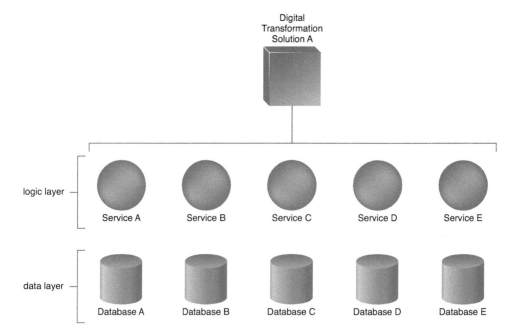

Figure 9.4

The services comprise the logic layer and the databases comprise the data layer. A given solution can be comprised of services and databases shared by other solutions in addition to dedicated services and databases.

Services have application programming interfaces (APIs). An API communicates the functions that a software program can carry out. It provides an interface that allows other programs to connect to and interact with the software program to carry out its functions.

An API essentially:

- enables communication, and…

- enables data exchange, and…

- …establishes rules and requirements for how communication and data exchange can occur.

Because digital transformation solutions are commonly built as distributed applications comprised of services, the focus is typically on APIs that are published as part of services, known as *service APIs*. Service APIs have *service capabilities* (Figure 9.5) that represent the functions that other programs can invoke.

TIP
So just to summarize: solutions have a logic layer comprised of services that are accessed via APIs, as well as a data layer primarily comprised of databases.

Service APIs act as endpoints that allow different services and software programs within the solution to communicate with each other, but also allow external software programs to communicate with the solution itself (Figure 9.6).

Figure 9.5
Each service exposes an API comprised of service capabilities. This enables other services and other software programs to issue requests for the service to carry out functions. For example, in this scenario, Service A acts as a consumer program that invokes Capability A of Service D.

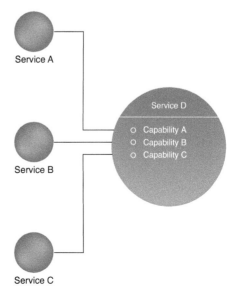

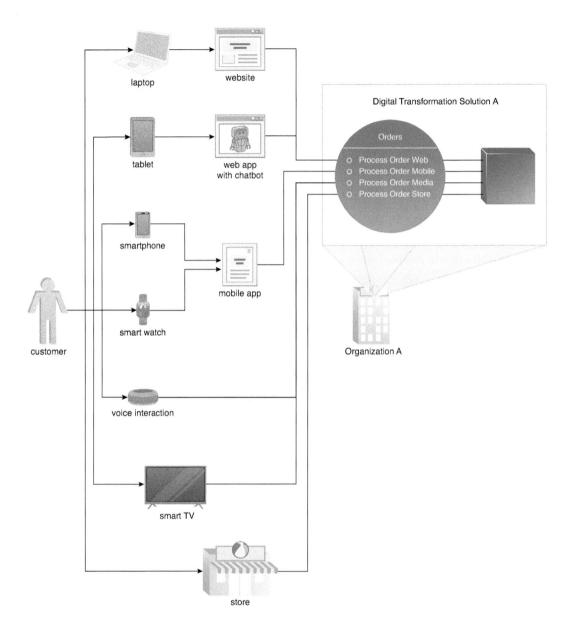

Figure 9.6

The ubiquitous multiexperience access scenario from Chapter 3 is revisited to highlight how it is supported via the Orders service API that acts as an external endpoint for Digital Transformation Solution A.

Data Ingress Basics

Within the context of digital transformation, *data ingress* is the act of bringing data into an organization. The opposite of data ingress is *data egress*, which is the act of getting data out of an organization.

When building digital transformation solutions, there is a great deal of emphasis on how and from where the large quantities of required data will be brought into the organization. This is why data ingress is a primary focal point.

When carrying out data ingress, many underlying technologies can be involved (such as transport, messaging and security technologies). The purpose of this section is not to document these underlying technologies, but to only highlight the following primary mechanisms used to carry out data ingress:

> **TIP**
>
> External data providers can push new data into an organization, or the organization can proactively pull the data in itself. The data ingress method used depends on the nature of the data, how frequently the organization needs it and the type of relationship it has with the data provider.

- File Pull

- File Push

- API Pull

- API Push

- Data Streaming

File Pull

With a File Pull approach, the organization retrieves files from a remote (and usually secured) location (Figure 9.7). A common example is the use of FTP or a shared cloud-based folder. A system may be employed to periodically pull any new files placed into the location. File pull systems are common with third-party data providers, especially from public sector data sources, such as government agencies.

Figure 9.7
A file pull being carried out by Organization A
whereby it retrieves new files placed into a shared
folder by Data Provider A.

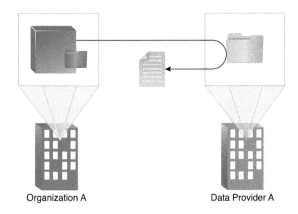

Organization A   Data Provider A

File Push

When a third-party data provider proactively places data files at a predetermined location for a recipient organization (Figure 9.8), a File Push is carried out. This approach
is applicable when the organization has a subscription with the data provider and also
when, in a private sector community, there is a pre-arranged data sharing system established among the community members.

Figure 9.8
A file push is initiated by Data Provider A, whereby it
places new files into a designated folder that belongs
to Organization A.

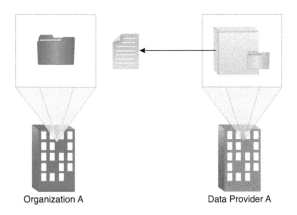

Organization A   Data Provider A

Unlike the File Pull model where organizations can retrieve the files at their convenience, a File Push usually places the responsibility on the data provider to get new files
out to those that are expecting them. This means that file transfer arrangements (including any necessary security arrangements) need to be made with all recipients ahead of
time. For cases where the file transmissions still unexpectedly fail, there may be the
need for the data provider to involve a queuing system that will automatically retry the
file transmissions on a periodic basis.

API Pull

When organizations require on-demand data from a data provider on a regular basis, it can be more efficient, more secure and more reliable to directly interface with data provider systems rather than to pull files or have files pushed to them.

This is accomplished through the use of APIs, whereby the organization has a consumer program (such as a service) that has been designed to create a connection with a provider program (which can also be a service). In this case, the program offered by the data provider has an API with capabilities that can be invoked by the consumer program to retrieve the data (Figure 9.9).

Figure 9.9
Organization A's service invokes the Get Data capability of a service from Data Provider A to retrieve the requested data on-demand. With this type of exchange, the actual data is usually packaged in messages that can be secured and equipped with additional metadata.

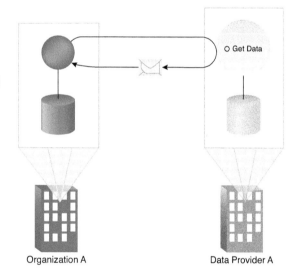

Organization A Data Provider A

The API Pull approach is common when organizations develop close (B2B) relationships with partner organizations or have on-going subscriptions with third-party data vendors.

API Push

An alternative to API Pull is API Push, whereby the data provider is responsible for initiating the data transmission by invoking the API of a program with the recipient organization (Figure 9.10). Similar to the File Push model, the API Push approach puts the responsibility of sharing new data with any designated recipient organizations upon the data provider.

Figure 9.10

Data Provider A's service invokes the Import Data
capability of a service API from Organization A in
order to provide it with new data.

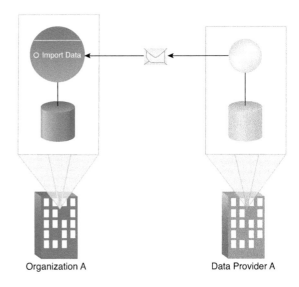

Organization A   Data Provider A

The data provider's program responsible for transmitting the data can utilize a messaging queue to periodically retry data transmissions.

Data Streaming

When a data provider can supply or generate new data on a frequent basis and when the organization requires that new data on a frequent basis, any of the preceding data ingress models will likely be inadequate. With the Data Streaming approach, a connection between the data provider and the recipient organization is established to facilitate the continuous streaming of data from the provider to the organization (Figure 9.11).

This approach is different from the API Push approach with regards to the duration for which a connection is established. When invoking an API, a connection is made only long enough to retrieve the requested data (usually just a few milliseconds) after which the connection is terminated until the next request. With Data Streaming, a persistent connection is established for longer periods of time (perhaps even indefinitely), until explicitly terminated. Specialized streaming programs are used to manage the data streaming reliably and with sufficient bandwidth allocation.

Figure 9.11

Organization A and Data Provider A have a data
streaming system set up that enables Data Provider A
to continually stream data to Organization A.

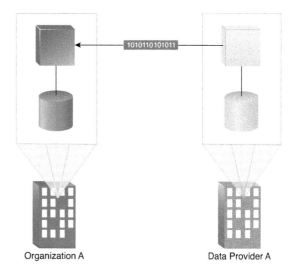

Organization A   Data Provider A

Data streaming (also referred to as *event streaming* when the source of data is event-related) is common when the solution needs to collect streams of telemetry data from IoT systems. An organization may also set up a data streaming relationship with an external data provider if it can offer streams of third-party data of value to the organization.

> **NOTE**
>
> Also worth noting is that data collected from different sources can exist in different formats, such as:
>
> - *Structured Data* – This is data that conforms to a data model or schema. It often exists in a tabular form and can be relational, meaning that data in one table can have a relationship with data in another table. Such data is often stored in relational databases.
>
> - *Unstructured Data* – When data exists in an inconsistent or non-relational format, it is considered to be unstructured. This type of data can be textual or binary. Examples include documents created using word processors, as well as image, audio and video files. Unstructured data can be stored in special repositories, such as NoSQL databases.
>
> - *Semi-Structured Data* – When a set of data has a defined structure but is not relational, it is considered semi-structured. Semi-structured data usually exists in a textual format. XML and JSON files are common examples, as well as data in emails and spreadsheets.
>
> These data formats are occasionally referenced in subsequent chapters.

Common Digital Transformation Technologies

Chapter 3: Common Technology Drivers introduced a set of technology innovations that, collectively, help realize digital transformation. Each of these technology drivers can support the attainment of one or more of the goals and benefits described in *Chapter 4: Common Benefits and Goals*. Each of these drivers can be further mapped to one or more specific technologies.

Understanding how individual technologies relate to and can help realize the common benefits of digital transformation can enable IT departments to identify which technologies may be necessary to attain the benefits relevant to their organization's business goals.

The next two chapters provide brief overviews of the following primary technologies:

* Cloud Computing

* Blockchain

* Internet of Things (IoT)

* Robotic Process Automation (RPA)

* Big Data Analysis and Analytics

* Machine Learning

* Artificial Intelligence (AI)

The final chaper in this book provides a detailed, step-by-step scenario that demonstrates the involvement of all of these technologies as part of a greater digital transformation solution.

To simplify upcoming illustrations and descriptions of how these technologies can be combined, the icons shown in Figure 9.12 will be used from hereon.

Figure 9.12

The icons used to represent the primary digital transformation technologies. From left to right: Cloud Computing, Blockchain, Internet of Things (IoT), Robotic Process Automation (RPA), Big Data, Machine Learning and Artificial Intelligence (AI).

How these technologies are associated with the previously described technology drivers is shown in Table 9.1.

Driver	Technology
Enhanced and Diverse Data Collection	Big Data, IoT, RPA
Contemporary Data Science	Big Data, Machine Learning, AI
Sophisticated Automation Technology	RPA
Autonomous Decision-Making	AI
Centralized, Scalable, Resilient IT Resources	Cloud Computing
Immutable Data Storage	Blockchain
Ubiquitous Multiexperience Access	Cloud Computing

Table 9.1
Each technology driver from Chapter 3 can be mapped to one or more of the primary technologies covered in Chapters 10 and 11.

Digital transformation solutions cannot be built with only these technologies. The focus is on those technology innovations closely associated with digital transformation because their collective usage is what commonly distinguishes digital transformation solutions from traditional (pre-digital transformation) solutions.

There are several additional technologies and practices that are important and even vital to building reliant and performant digital transformation solutions, including:

- Contemporary UI/UX Design

- Cybersecurity

- DevOps

- Microservices

- Containerization

- Service API Design & Management

- Service-Oriented Architecture (SOA)

TIP
Microservices, containerization, APIs and SOA are explored in other titles in the *Pearson Digital Enterprise Series from Thomas Erl.*

> **NOTE**
>
> As previously mentioned, the next two chapters are dedicated to introducing the seven primary digital transformation technologies. It is important to note that these chapters do not cover the technologies completely or comprehensively. Their purpose is to clarify the relevance of a given technology to digital transformation and to highlight key considerations, risks and challenges.

Chapter 10

An Introduction to Digital Transformation Automation Technologies

Cloud Computing

Blockchain

Internet of Things (IoT)

Robotic Process Automation (RPA)

Much better!

*Digital transformation solutions can take automation to a whole new
level, not only by incorporating modern automation innovations,
but also by taking advantage of available data intelligence to
better determine what can be effectively automated and how that
automation can be best carried out. Let's sit back and learn about
how new opportunities to automate things can improve our lives.*

Enhancing an organization's automation capabilities is a core objective of digital transformation, both in terms of improving customer-centricity, as well as optimizing the organization's internal operations.

This chapter provides introductory coverage of the following automation technologies:

- Cloud Computing

- Blockchain

- Internet of Things (IoT)

- Robotic Process Automation (RPA)

Each technology is briefly introduced, with an emphasis of highlighting its relationship with digital transformation and the creation of customer-centric solutions (Figure 10.1).

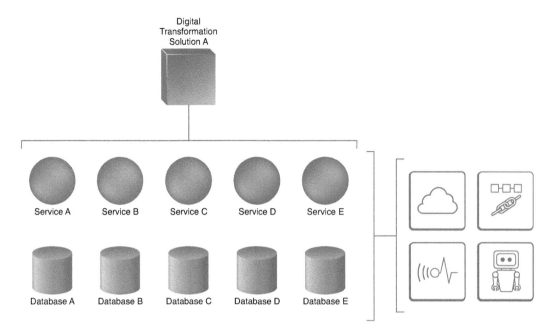

Figure 10.1
The four key automation technologies can relate to and impact both the logic and data layers of a digital transformation solution.

Cloud Computing

Cloud computing is a specialized form of distributed computing that introduces utilization models for remotely provisioning scalable and measured IT resources. What this means is that cloud computing technology provides the ability to centralize large pools of IT infrastructure resources (such as physical servers, virtual servers, databases, etc.) that can be used to support the processing requirements of numerous solutions.

Cloud Computing in Practice

Contemporary cloud computing technology is powerful and sophisticated and is considered a core underlying part of many digital transformation environments. Some primary features of clouds relevant to digital transformation solutions include:

TIP
Another common benefit is the option to defer the administration and maintenance responsibilities of your servers, databases and other IT resources to the cloud provider.

- The ability to support on-demand scaling of IT resources so that high concurrent usage and unexpected usage volumes can be readily and automatically accommodated.

- The ability to provide extensive failover support so that if some or all parts of a digital transformation solution should fail, underlying mechanisms automatically provision new instances of those resources, thereby allowing the solution to continue operating as normal.

- The ability to measure usage for administrative and billing purposes. An organization can lease a cloud environment and only be billed for the actual usage of the IT resources its solution consumes. When required, the resource allocation for a given digital transformation solution can be limited and controlled.

An organization does not need to place its entire digital transformation solution inside a cloud in order to benefit from these features. It can choose to only have a subset of the solution components residing in a cloud (Figure 10.2).

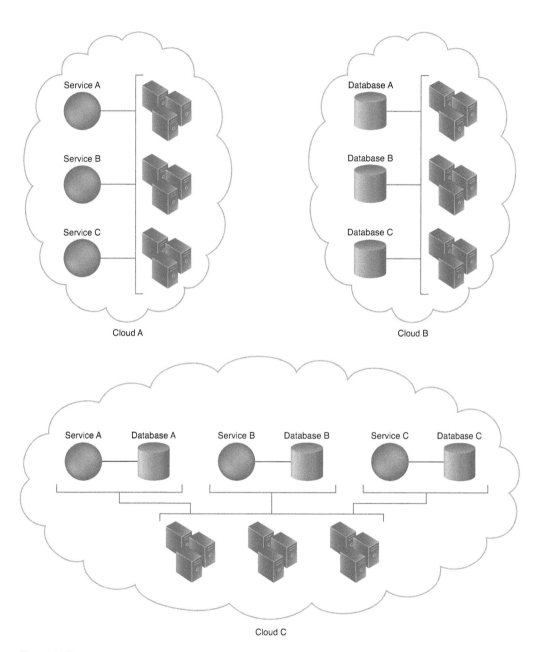

Figure 10.2

Each of these clouds demonstrates a different deployment option for a subset of components of Digital Transformation Solution A from Figure 10.1. Cloud A hosts three of the five solution services, whereas Cloud B hosts three of the five solution databases. In Cloud C, three services are hosted together with three databases. (The blue boxes are the servers in the cloud that are hosting the services and databases.)

Figures 10.3, 10.4 and 10.5 take a closer look at how and where the solution's five services and databases could be physically distributed in relation to Clouds A, B and C.

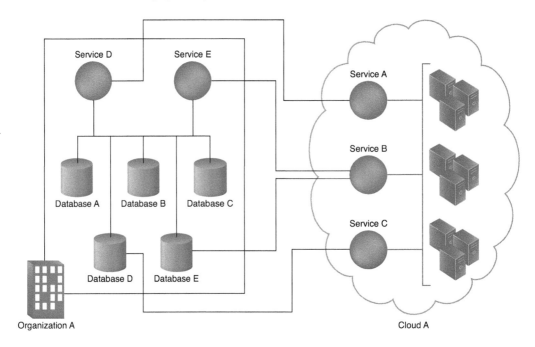

Figure 10.3

All five databases reside on-premise within Organization A, while three services are hosted in an external cloud environment (Cloud A). This may be a suitable model for when Services A, B and C are subjected to high or unpredictable periods of concurrent usage, in which case the cloud environment will automatically scale the required underlying IT resources accordingly.

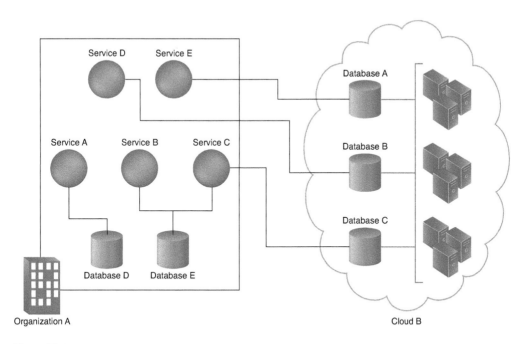

Figure 10.4
All five services reside on-premise within Organization A, while three databases are hosted in an external cloud environment (Cloud B). This may be a suitable model for when Databases A, B and C have high volume storage requirements or may be subject to high volumes of concurrent data access (such as by machine learning or AI systems). In this case, the cloud environment can provide automatic replication and synchronization of databases to support high usage and processing demands.

As referenced in the caption for Figure 10.5, there may be policies and regulations that can make external cloud environments provided by third-party vendors unsuitable or incompatible with some or all parts of a given solution. This is especially true for digital transformation solutions due to their data-centric nature and their reliance on the access to and processing of large volumes of data sources. Strict data privacy and protection regulations can make it impossible for any part of such solutions to reside outside of organizational boundaries. This is why *private* clouds are common foundations for digital transformation environments.

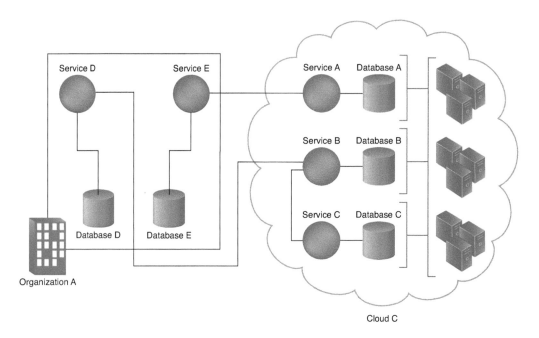

Figure 10.5

Two services and two databases reside on-premise in Organization A, while three services and three databases are hosted in an external cloud environment (Cloud C). This model may be suitable when a distinct part of the overall digital transformation requires high performance and/or high reliability, both of which can be provided on-demand by the underlying cloud environment. The services and databases residing within the organization may not have high performance or reliability requirements or may be required to stay within organizational boundaries in order to comply with certain policies and regulations.

A private cloud is a cloud that is physically located within an organization's IT enterprise. The organization's IT division owns the cloud environment and has a central group of IT staff responsible for managing it. Its resources are then shared with project teams from other IT departments that are building or extending individual automation solutions (Figure 10.6).

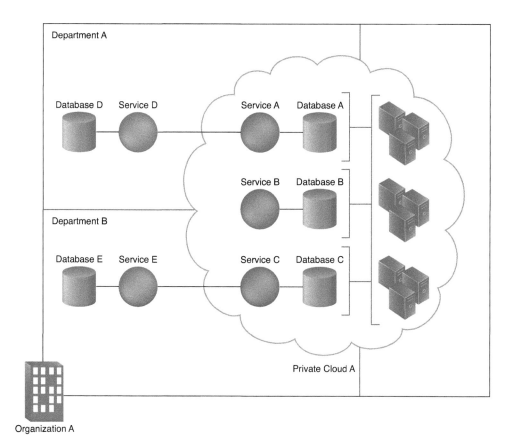

Figure 10.6
An organization provides a private cloud to host a pool of scalable and resilient IT resources in support of the digital solutions from different organization departments.

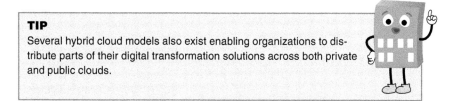

TIP
Several hybrid cloud models also exist enabling organizations to distribute parts of their digital transformation solutions across both private and public clouds.

Common Risks and Challenges

- *Increased Security Vulnerabilities* – The remote location of the resources provided by public clouds requires an expansion of trust boundaries that can be difficult to establish without introducing security concerns. Furthermore, hosting solution logic and business data in public clouds may raise security vulnerabilities outside of the organization's control or may introduce the need for integrated security frameworks.

- *Reduced Operational Governance Control* – Organizations that use public clouds are commonly given a lower level of control over cloud-based infrastructure when compared to the control they have over their own internal IT infrastructure. This reduced level of control forms a direct dependency on the cloud provider, which can introduce risk when the cloud provider is unreliable.

- *Limited Portability Between Cloud Providers* – Due to a lack of accepted industry standards within the cloud computing industry, individual public cloud environments can be somewhat proprietary. Forming dependencies on these environments can make it difficult for organizations to move their IT assets to another cloud.

- *Multi-Regional Compliance and Legal Issues* – When hosting data in a public cloud, the actual physical location of the data could end up being in a geographical region that violates data-related industry or government regulations and policies.

TIP
While the first four listed risks and challenges are primarily associated with the use of public clouds, the last item is a risk that applies to both public and private clouds.

- *Cost Overruns* – While the primary justification for most cloud initiatives is to establish an environment that adds value by streamlining IT operations and reducing overhead and operational cost, the opposite can occur when cloud projects are not properly planned, carried out and governed.

Blockchain

Blockchain is a technology focused on the transparent and secure storage of important data.

Specifically, a blockchain system can do the following:

- Provide a means by which data records are stored in a highly secured repository, referred to as a *distributed ledger*. The distributed ledger provides "immutable" storage, which means that once the data is written to the database, the expectation is that it can never be altered.

- Allow for the distributed ledger to be owned or managed by multiple parties, instead of just one party. This is known as *decentralized authority* and it relies on the use of a comprehensive validation process (referred to as a *consensus* process) involving some or all users. This may be especially important for when blockchain is used in a community environment.

- Allow for transactions to be carried out between parties without the need for a central authority, such as a bank. This is the basis of cryptocurrency systems that utilize blockchain technology specifically for financial transactions.

- Enable all data to be transparent to all users. A blockchain environment can be comprised of a network in which users receive a complete or partial version of the entire distributed ledger. This type of open transparency is important for supporting decentralized authority.

Blockchain in Practice

While blockchain's origins are tied to the financial industry and the advent of cryptocurrencies, its actual usage within digital transformation environments has broadened. Its ability to provide highly secure data storage has made blockchain valuable to IT enterprises in different industries that need to provide immutable storage for critical business data of any kind (Figure 10.7).

Figure 10.7

A digital transformation solution's services access and store business data in different repositories. Service C stores important data into an immutable blockchain distributed ledger.

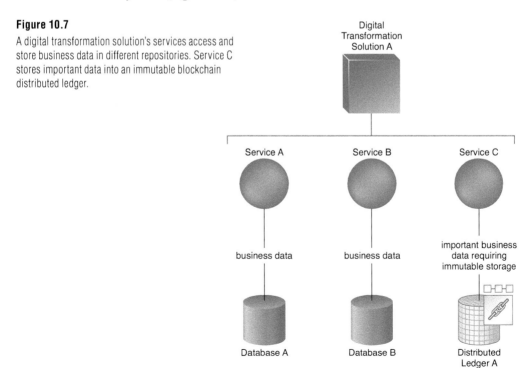

Within a distributed ledger, information is organized into blocks that are populated with data records and metadata. When a block reaches its capacity, it is added to an existing chain of blocks to which it becomes permanently linked through sophisticated security hashing methods (Figure 10.8).

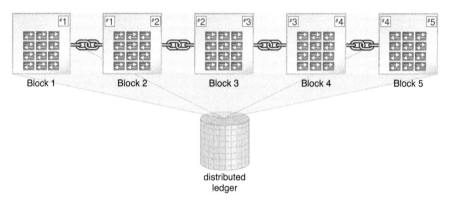

Figure 10.8
Within a distributed ledger, each block is linked together to form a chain of blocks (or a "blockchain").

Some sample scenarios for which blockchain may be suitable include:

• Financial transaction data that needs to be accurately recorded and safely persisted for future auditing purposes.

• Time-sensitive medical research and patient data that needs to be captured in immutable storage so that it can be reliably used for future medical research and treatments.

• Historical user access information that needs to be reliably logged to prevent it from being modified by malicious users and to ensure the integrity of future security audits.

• Business data and documents that need to be securely stored and timestamped for legal purposes so that the historical accuracy of the data is irrefutable in a court of law.

The decentralized and transparent usage model offered by blockchain can be used in partner communities to reliably share data and carry out transactions. However, private organizations that bring blockchain into their IT enterprises are not required to adopt this model. Blockchain systems can be built so that all users are under the control of the organization.

The distributed ledger provided by a blockchain system is designed specifically to provide immutable and highly secure data storage. It is less accommodating when it comes to subsequent data access and queries. Although tools providing data access to distributed ledgers exist, overall they are not as easily accessed as traditional relational databases.

As a result, there is a set of common co-existence models to enable organizations to position the distributed ledger within their digital transformation solutions depending on their requirements.

NOTE

The relational databases in the upcoming model descriptions are referred to as "centralized" to indicate that they are single databases accessed by multiple users. This is in contrast to a blockchain network whereby the "decentralized" distributed ledger can be redundantly copied for each user.

Partial Business Data Capture

A subset of data residing in a relational database can be redundantly stored in a distributed ledger (Figure 10.9). This model may be suitable when some of the data generated by a solution with a centralized database is considered sensitive or high value and for which long-term integrity needs to be preserved. In this case, the distributed ledger can be positioned as an immutable data store responsible for locking the data, as first captured, by ensuring that it can no longer be modified.

For example, the owners of an order processing solution may want the order transaction records to be redundantly captured in the distributed ledger, while all of the customer and product records can remain only in the relational database.

Figure 10.9

A portion of the data in a centralized relational database is redundantly captured in a distributed ledger.

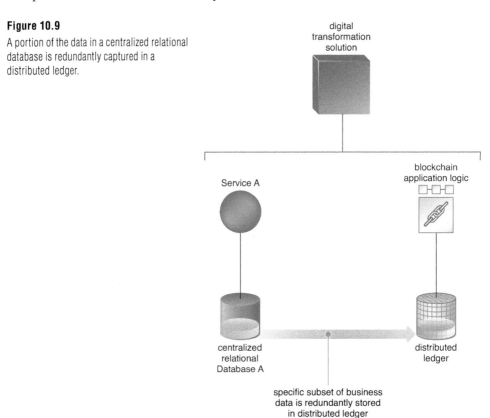

Full Business Data Capture

Most or all of the data in a relational database can be redundantly stored in a distributed ledger (Figure 10.10). This model is not common, but may be considered if the entire contents of a relational database need to be immutably stored and secured.

Figure 10.10

A majority of the data in a centralized database is redundantly captured in a distributed ledger.

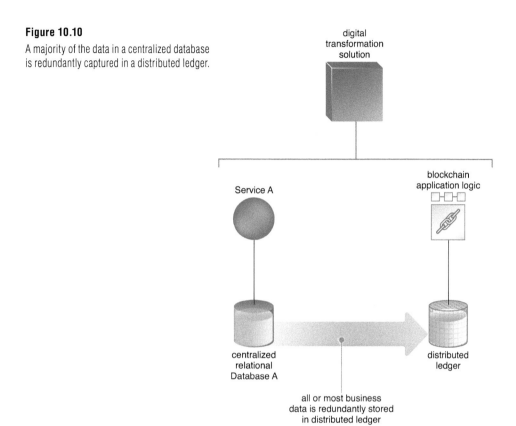

For example, a database in a police station may be dedicated to storing records pertaining to evidence collected at crime scenes, including the names of the police personnel that located, processed and stored the evidence, as well as the IDs of personnel that checked items of evidence in and out of storage. The contents of this database may be considered important enough to warrant its entire capture in a distributed ledger so that all associated records are permanently and immutably stored.

Log Data Access Capture

The data access log information of a centralized relational database can be captured in the distributed ledger (Figure 10.11). This model may be suitable for enhancing the security control over a business database so that if there is ever any question about unauthorized data access attempts or data manipulation that may have occurred, the immutable log repository provided by the distributed ledger can be checked as a reliable "source of truth."

Figure 10.11

The historical data access log records for a centralized relational database are stored in the distributed ledger.

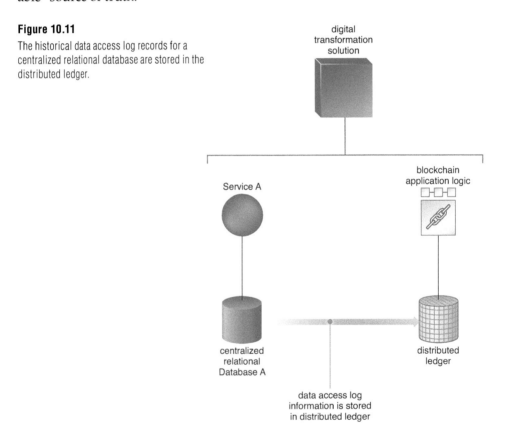

For example, a university may have a database containing student records with grades and achieved accreditations. This database is used to maintain and verify each student's academic status. Security breaches may have occurred, whereby attempts were made to retroactively change grades or achieved accreditations and further manipulate historical log data. Some of these breaches may have gone undetected for periods of time. Using the immutable data access log records in the corresponding distributed ledger, reliable historical audits can be carried out to identify and detect irregular and suspicious data access activity.

Partial Business Data Store

A business solution stores a portion of its data in a centralized relational database and other data in a distributed ledger (Figure 10.12). This model aims to avoid unnecessary redundancy of data across the relational database and the distributed ledger. Records with high performance data access requirements (such as create, read, update and delete actions) are stored in the centralized relational database. Records that require formal validation and permanent and immutable storage are placed into the distributed ledger. This model can still be augmented to allow for subsets of either repository to be redundantly stored.

Figure 10.12

A service is integrated with a blockchain system as part of the same overall digital transformation solution. At runtime, the solution logic determines whether records should be stored in the centralized relational database or submitted to the blockchain system logic for storage in the distributed ledger.

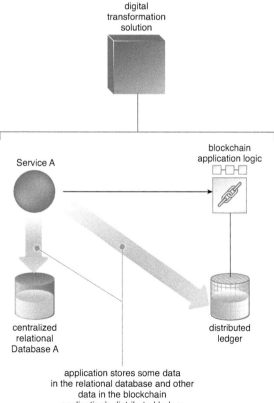

For example, a regulatory organization responsible for processing vehicle insurance claims may have a solution used to store a range of records associated with vehicle damage and personal injury claims. Police reports received at the accident scene are submitted to the organization and then transcribed by a clerk. Each police report is considered private, whereas the transcribed version is made available to those involved with the claim.

The solution can be designed so that police report records are submitted directly to the distributed ledger and the public versions of the reports, as well as other claims-related records, are stored in the central relational database. Should there ever be a dispute regarding the legitimacy of the public accident report data, the original police report data can be retrieved from the distributed ledger, acting as a reliable "source of truth."

Ledger Export

Data records residing in the distributed ledger are exported to a centralized relational database (Figure 10.13). This model may be suitable for when the data collected by a blockchain system needs to be made available in a more data access-friendly manner. Depending on the nature of the data and the functional requirements of those accessing the data via the relational database, this model may introduce complexity with how records should be structured in relational database tables.

For example, a popular financial blockchain system may have collected years of transaction history. The community that participates and oversees the decentralized blockchain network collectively decides to launch a new financial solution based on a new form of cryptocurrency. Before doing so, they would like to be able to do some analysis work with the historical data from their existing solution to produce a series of reports, including reports based on big data analytics and predictive modeling.

In support of this research, a relational database can be established containing the relevant data exported from the distributed ledger and arranged in a relational data model for the planned analysis project. Users can safely update and augment the data for reporting purposes, knowing that the original historical data records are still secured in the current blockchain system's distributed ledger.

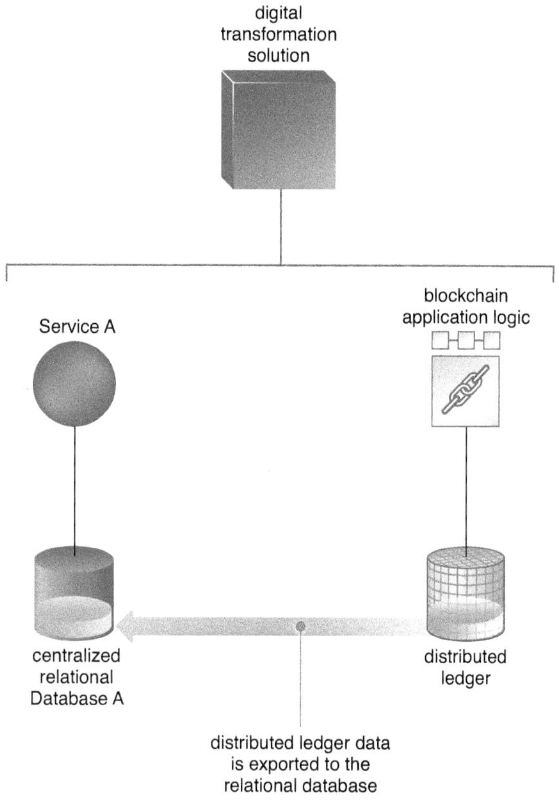

Figure 10.13

Records in a distributed ledger are exported to redundantly reside in a centralized relational database.

digital
transformation
solution

Service A

blockchain
application logic

centralized
relational
Database A

distributed
ledger

distributed ledger data
is exported to the
relational database

Common Risks and Challenges

- *Security Loopholes* – Blockchains used within a community can rely on a voting system, meaning that if a malicious party were to gain control over the majority of votes, it may be able to purposely validate forged or invalid records.

- *Data Privacy Concerns* – Community blockchain systems can be designed to be permissionless, allowing potentially private data to be openly viewed and accessed.

- *Wasteful Processing* – Some blockchain processing requirements can demand significant compute power, resulting in exorbitant and potentially wasteful energy consumption.

- *Scalability Thresholds* – Some blockchain system designs can place restrictions on the validation and creation of blocks. These restrictions can inhibit the overall scalability of the system, which may be relevant depending on how quickly an organization may need to write and access data.

- *Illegal Activity* – Because a blockchain system can be used to circumvent a central authority, it may be more susceptible to being abused for illegal purposes.

- *Difficult to Integrate* – A blockchain system is primarily designed to be a standalone implementation. Its underlying technology is distinct and therefore different than conventional automation solution technology. This can make integrating blockchain systems within an IT enterprise potentially costly and complex.

TIP
The Security Loopholes, Data Privacy Concerns, Scalability Thresholds and Illegal Activity risks and challenges are more applicable when blockchain is used within a community.

The last item on this list relates back to the co-existence models covered earlier and further highlights the need for careful planning as to how a blockchain system and its distributed ledger needs to be positioned and incorporated within an IT enterprise.

Internet of Things (IoT)

IoT is a field of technology dedicated to establishing broad connectivity in support of positioning devices capable of remotely collecting telemetry data and carrying out commands.

An IoT system consists of a collection of devices connected by a network that may rely on gateways, telecommunications towers and satellites to cover a geographical range. While the scope of a given IoT system can be moderate (comprised of a handful of devices in a single location), many IoT systems are very large, comprising hundreds of devices spread across many locations.

IoT Devices

IoT devices are hardware components with their own power source. Each device has a modem used to receive and transmit data. A device may further contain one or more sensors, one or more actuators and control logic (Figure 10.14).

Figure 10.14

IoT devices can be set up with different combinations of capabilities to carry out different types of functions.

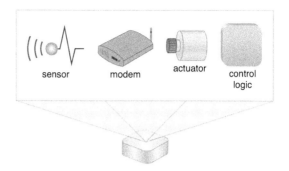

Sensors are used to remotely collect data about specific activities. The IoT device then uses its *modem* to transmit this data back to the digital transformation solution. This type of remotely collected and transmitted data is referred to as *telemetry data* (Figure 10.15).

TIP
IoT sensors are often designed with very small electrical components that can operate for long periods of time on low amounts of battery power. Some devices can stay powered for years on a single battery.

IoT systems can generate a large quantity of telemetry data, which can be streamed continuously or in intervals. Telemetry data is most commonly used as input for a digital transformation platform's data science systems (Figure 10.16). These systems can continually analyze and process the latest telemetry data in support of solution capabilities and/or to provide data intelligence for manual or automated decision-making.

The IoT device's modem may be further able to receive commands from the digital transformation solution. Such devices are equipped with *actuators* that are capable of interacting with physical objects (Figure 10.17).

Figure 10.15

A utility worker needs to drive to each home to take a meter reading (top). This manual process consumes significant time and effort because the meter gauge cannot be remotely accessed. When the house is equipped with an IoT device with a sensor, an in-person visit from a human utility worker is no longer required (bottom). The IoT system further provides the solution with a more current and accurate view of usage over time so that it can be more responsive in aligning supply with demand.

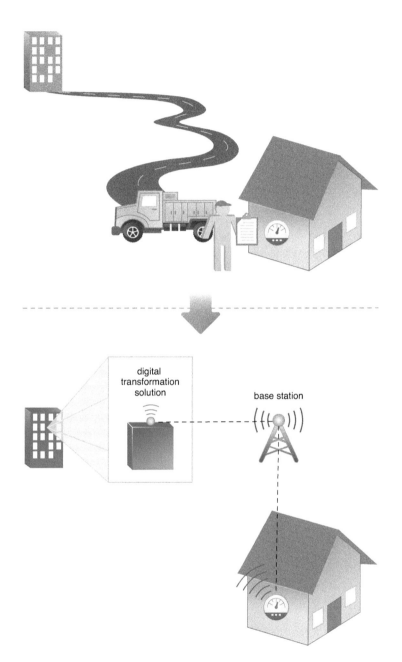

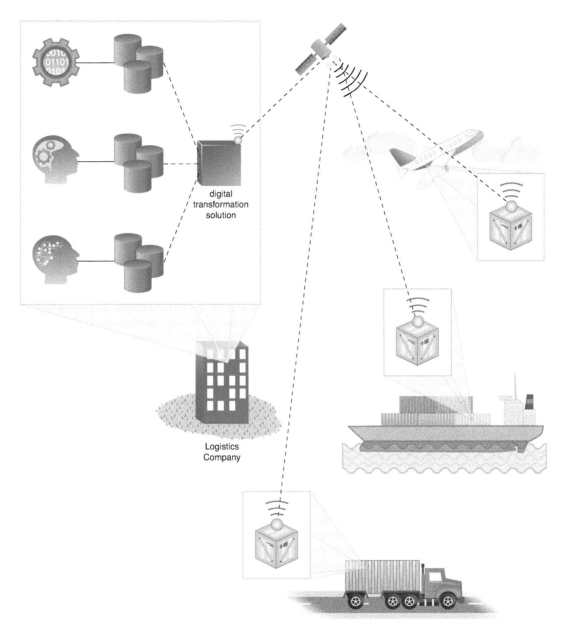

Figure 10.16
A logistics company receives constant telemetry data streams from IoT devices. This data is used to track different assets being shipped internationally. Back-end analysis and processing systems further analyze this data to constantly assess the performance of individual transportation methods and to identify potential opportunities for optimizations and improvements.

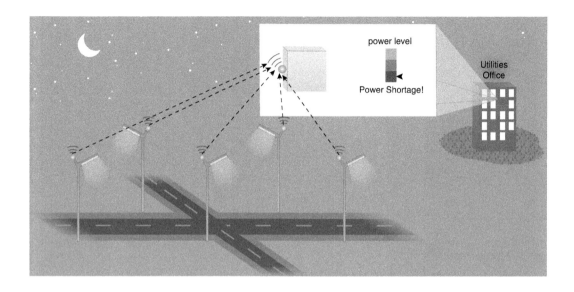

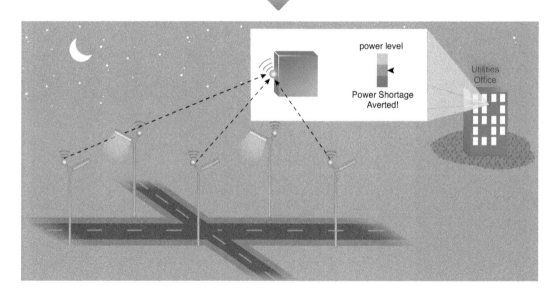

Figure 10.17

The streetlights in a city are pre-programmed to turn on and off at specific times. When the Utilities Office encounters an energy shortage, the streetlights remain on, contributing to the decrease in available power (top). With a digital transformation solution in place, the streetlights are equipped with IoT devices that have actuators enabling the lights to be remotely and individually turned on and off. In the depicted scenario the solution responds to a power shortage by sending commands to temporarily turn off every other streetlight (bottom). The decision to send this command may have originated with a human worker or an AI system.

An IoT device can further contain *control logic* that does not require that it receive commands from the back-end solution. Instead, the control logic enables it to process sensor data locally and carry out internal logic to issue commands to the actuator (Figure 10.18).

Figure 10.18

An airplane transports cargo that includes a refrigeration unit holding perishable goods. An IoT device attached to the refrigeration unit is capable of self-monitoring the refrigeration temperature. The device's control logic detects if the temperature level falls too low or goes too high. When necessary, it independently invokes the actuator to adjust the refrigeration temperature.

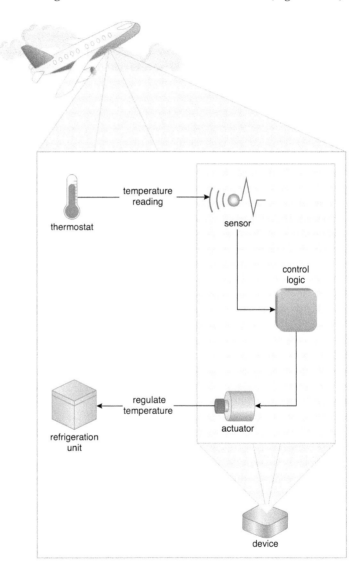

IoT in Practice

Depending on the nature of an organization's business and its interactions with customers, IoT systems can be a significant contributor to improving customer-centricity. IoT systems are common parts of "smart" solutions for homes and offices where they can be used to proactively detect and resolve problems (Figure 10.19) and improve the convenience of customers and the productivity of personnel responsible for supporting customers.

TIP

Industrial IoT (or IIoT) is a specialized variation of IoT not focused so much on customer interactions, but more on collecting telemetry data from industrial environments, such as manufacturing plants.

IoT systems can be very large. Some are comprised of hundreds of devices that continually collect and process telemetry data. Entire communities can utilize IoT systems to optimize broad infrastructures and operational environments. The back-end digital transformation solution receiving telemetry data and issuing commands to devices can even be in another geographical region altogether (Figure 10.20).

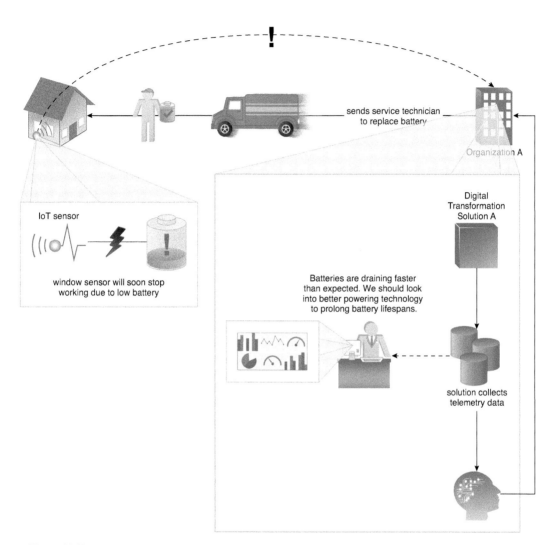

Figure 10.19

The scenario shown previously in the *Telemetry Data Capture* section in Chapter 7 is revisited to further illustrate how an AI system automates the decision to dispatch a service technician, and how the collected data is further added to the data intelligence used to support manual intelligent decision-making.

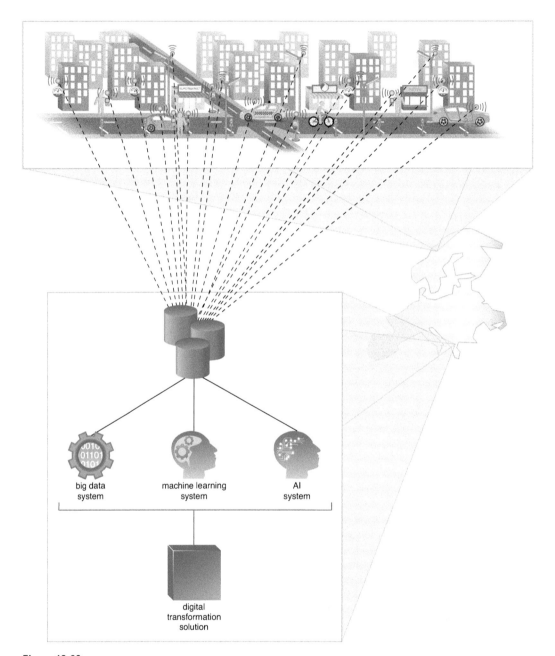

Figure 10.20

A digital transformation solution located in one region collects and processes urban activity data received from an IoT system in a different region. The solution could be owned by a government that receives this type of data from different cities across different regions. The data may be analyzed by the government agency to determine how different urban environments can be further improved for their residents (customers). The data may also be made available as public sector data for use by other organizations who may find it relevant to improving their businesses.

> **TIP**
> IoT is also a core technology that enables *digital twin* solutions, whereby a physical object (such as a vehicle or a manufacturing machine) can be recreated virtually using sensor data collected from the real object. This allows the digital twin to be subjected to different simulated scenarios so that improvements can be made and tested before actually doing so on the real object. The data collected from these simulations can be further fed into data science systems for analysis and training purposes.

Common Risks and Challenges

- *Complex Ecosystem* – IoT systems can evolve into large and complex environments comprised of a multitude of connected devices, middleware and network connections. This can lead to burdensome maintenance and governance responsibilities.

- *Lack of Standardization* – The IoT industry is comprised of a diverse range of connectivity options available across all communication layers. The lack of industry standardization can lead to disparate IoT systems being built upon proprietary architectures incompatible with each other. This can result in significant interoperability challenges for when different systems need to be connected.

- *Cost vs. Value of Connectivity* – When planning an IoT delivery project, it can be difficult to predict just how many devices may need to be connected and the extent of interactivity that may need to occur across those devices to support the range of usage scenarios that may be required. As a result, it can be correspondingly challenging to predict the actual cost of building and running an IoT-based environment. If the resulting cost turns out to exceed the value provided by the IoT system, then it will not adequately fulfill the business goals it was intended to help achieve.

- *Data Privacy Regulation* – The nature of data collected by different devices may be subject to regional data privacy regulations that may limit the extent to which the data can be shared, transmitted and stored by digital transformation solutions. Given the potential volume of data that can be collected, this can be difficult to monitor and control.

> **CAUTION**
> Another potential issue, especially with IoT devices that are geographically dispersed, is their communication of telemetry data via low-band networks. Connectivity issues can cause telemetry data to be streamed at inconsistent intervals.

- *Security Enforcement* – IoT devices often need to operate in a resource-constrained mode. This can make it challenging to incorporate the processing requirements to encrypt and otherwise secure transmitted data, especially in high volumes. Unsecured data predictably becomes vulnerable to unauthorized access and potential abuse.

- *Collecting "Noisy" Data* – A key success factor of any IoT system that is part of a greater digital transformation environment is ensuring that the nature of the data being collected is correctly defined. It is very easy for IoT systems to inadvertently collect large quantities of irrelevant data that simply add "noise" that data science systems end up having to filter out.

Robotic Process Automation (RPA)

Robotic Process Automation (RPA) is a business process automation technology used specifically to automate tasks that are traditionally carried out manually by humans.

RPA utilizes specialized software programs (commonly referred to as *bots*) that are programmed to act as virtual workers capable of interacting with user interfaces originally designed for use by humans (Figure 10.21).

Figure 10.21
Although depicted as a robot, RPA bots are actually specialized software programs designed to duplicate tasks that are normally carried out by humans using a computer.

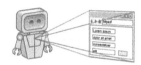

Depending on the nature of manual tasks being carried out, the deployment of RPA within an organization can result in dramatic productivity improvements. A single RPA bot may be able to carry out a set of redundant and predictable tasks in the same amount of time that it could take a group of humans to do so (Figure 10.22).

manual data entry by humans

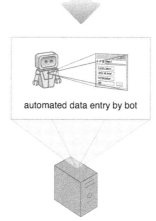

automated data entry by bot

Figure 10.22
A single RPA bot may be able to equal the productivity of multiple human workers.

RPA in Practice

The most common types of tasks automated by RPA are administrative tasks that involve repetitive actions.

Some examples include:

- *Data Entry* – RPA bots can read or retrieve data and then interact with online forms to populate and submit data.

- *Message Routing* – RPA bots can read and process data being received, such as data sent via email, and then extract portions of that data to be routed to others (also via email).

- *Web Searching* – RPA bots can interact with web browsers to scan websites and collect different types of data. The bots can aggregate and consolidate this data before storing it or forwarding it further.

- *Data Searching and Management* – RPA can be used to organize data and files. For example, the RPA bots may open files to extract data and then relocate the extracted data elsewhere. Bots may perform searches across files and documents to identify those that match search criteria and may further automate digitization via OCR to generate new digital data to search and organize.

- *User Acceptance Testing* – When solutions are created or updated, they generally need to undergo a testing phase during which humans try out a solution via available user interfaces. RPA bots can perform this type of user testing and can often do so more vigorously to try to root out any hard-to-find glitches.

The ability of RPA bots to interact with user interfaces is referred to as *front-end integration*, as it establishes a means of connecting with the front end of a system. RPA environments further support back-end integration, which means they are capable of connecting to systems via their APIs. Whereas the bots are responsible for front-end integration, a separate RPA controller program is typically responsible for the back-end integration (Figure 10.23).

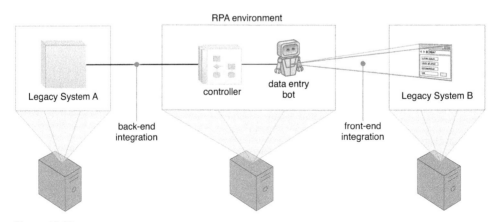

Figure 10.23
The RPA controller retrieves data from a legacy system by connecting to its API. The RPA bot receives the retrieved data and then uses it to populate a user interface on a different legacy system.

Regardless of the nature of the task they are automating, RPA bots have the ability to access and process a broad range of data (Figure 10.24). Data resulting from one task may then be used by the bot to complete another task.

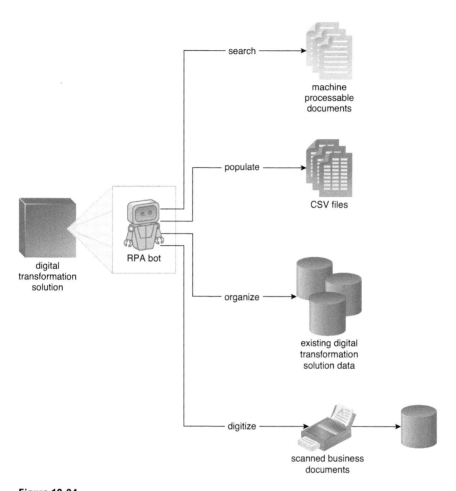

Figure 10.24

The RPA bot performs different data processing tasks on different types of data. These may be individual tasks that are repetitively automated, or they could be tasks completed sequentially as part of a workflow. To carry any of these tasks out, the bot would typically interact with a corresponding user interface (not shown in this figure).

Multiple RPA bots can be teamed up and orchestrated as part of a greater business process to work together. This may be suitable for a business process that requires the completion of two or more different manual tasks, each of which can be automated using RPA (Figure 10.25).

Figure 10.25

A routing bot that scans an email inbox to look for specific email messages. Depending on their contents, data may be extracted from the emails and forwarded to a human worker, a database or a separate data entry bot that uses the received data to carry out data entry tasks. The RPA controller logic orchestrates the involvement of the two bots.

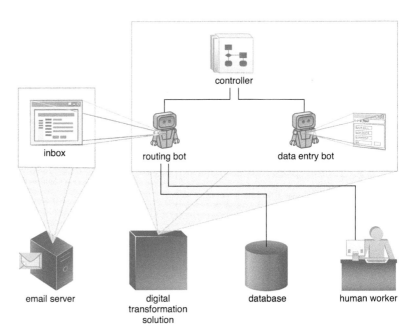

What further distinguishes RPA bots from regular software programs is that they are often made available as out-of-the-box programs that require little-to-no programming knowledge to configure and set up. RPA tools typically provide graphical user interfaces and simple scripting functions to make it relatively easy for non-technical users to enable a bot's front-end integration capabilities.

TIP
Combining RPA with data science technologies is also known as *hyperautomation*.

While bots can be set up to automate a range of simple tasks, RPA also has a relationship with artificial intelligence that can lead to a more sophisticated form of bot-driven business process automation known as *intelligent automation*. An AI system can carry out realtime automated decision-making to autonomously instruct RPA environments to perform different tasks and to further augment those instructions when adapting to new circumstances.

Common Risks and Challenges

- *Weak Integrations* – While RPA provides a means of establishing a bridge between the back end of one system and the front end of another, the benefits of doing so can be short-term only. It may sometimes be more effective to replace or enhance legacy environments to connect in a more direct and robust manner rather than to rely on an RPA environment to act as an intermediary. Over time, the use of RPA for this purpose can result in weak and fragile integrations between systems that can become unreliable and costly to maintain, thereby decreasing their long-term value.

- *Hidden Impacts* – The assignment of tasks (previously completed manually) to a bot that can now automate them can significantly alter the behavior, performance and complexion of the underlying business process. This may require that the business process itself be remodeled in order to ensure that it will continue to be carried out correctly. This remodeling effort can lead to further unexpected effort and costs.

- *Cultural and Ethical Concerns* – How the introduction of RPA bots is received in organizations will vary. Some organizations will make a genuine effort to plan for this type of transition so that those employees who had been previously completing the manual tasks to be automated by bots will be retrained and given more meaningful tasks to carry out. In other cases, there may be grave concerns about organizations downsizing when the usage of bots proves more economical than retaining human workers. Cultural impacts and ethical concerns cannot be underestimated as they may end up undermining the value gained by adopting RPA.

- *Performance Limitations* – RPA bots can be simple to set up and activate and can be very good at automating predictable tasks. However, some business process tasks are not always simple or predictable. Dealing with exceptions, changes or unforeseen conditions can lead bots to fail at completing some tasks or even skip tasks entirely, leaving them incomplete or unresolved.

- *Scaling Limitations* – As a result of the aforementioned performance limitations and the often unforeseen complexity of business processes that bots may find themselves participating in, it can be difficult to scale the utilization of bots in response to actual usage demands.

> **CAUTION**
> Some organizations fail to properly plan for the introduction of bots, which can lead to unexpected problems. Adding RPA bots will naturally change the complexion of a business process. Starting a project by re-engineering the workflow to accommodate the involvement of the bots can reduce the risk of these problems.

Chapter 11

An Introduction to
Digital Transformation
Data Science Technologies

Big Data Analysis and Analytics

Machine Learning

Artificial Intelligence (AI)

As we've emphasized throughout the chapters so far, much of what distinguishes digital transformation and much of what determines its success comes down to data intelligence. Here, we finally get to take a closer look at the data science innovations that can make the creation of intelligent data a reality.

Data intelligence is the lifeblood of digital transformation environments. Both automation solutions and human decision makers rely on the enhanced quality and speed at which data intelligence can be provided in order to improve customer-centricity and to help strategically guide the business overall.

This chapter provides introductory coverage of the following data science technologies:

- Big Data Analysis and Analytics

- Machine Learning

- Artificial Intelligence (AI)

As with the previous chapter, the coverage of the technologies is primarily focused on how the technologies relate to digital transformation and how they are used to provide data intelligence for decision makers (Figure 11.1).

 ## Big Data Analysis and Analytics

As referenced previously, digital transformation environments are inherently data-driven and are expected to amass large quantities of data that will continue to accumulate on an on-going basis.

Big data analysis and analytics (or just *big data*) is an established field of data science that encompasses the data analytics, analysis, processing and storage of large collections of disparate data for the purpose of producing new forms of data intelligence (Figure 11.2).

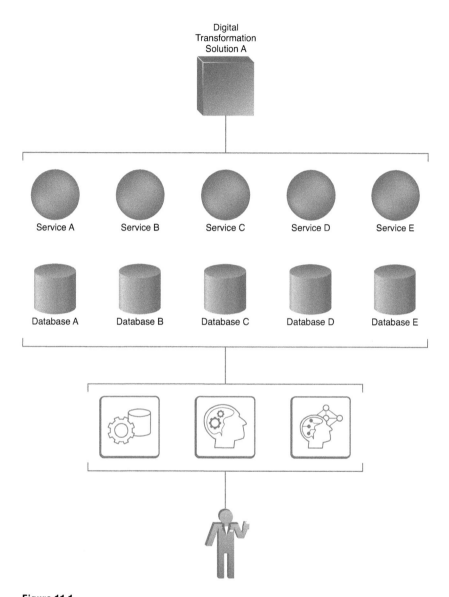

Figure 11.1

The three key data science technologies relate to the data layer of digital transformation solutions as well as human decision makers.

Figure 11.2

A glimpse into a typical big data system. It is capable of receiving (ingesting) differently structured data from different sources and subjecting that data to a series of processing steps that produce data intelligence, meaningful results used by a decision maker.

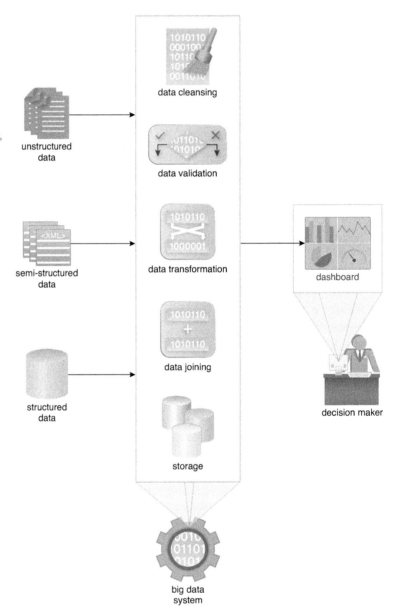

The field of big data is comprised of practices and technologies that leverage and build upon traditional data science techniques and carry over into other contemporary data science fields (such as machine learning and AI).

Big data systems can be used to:

- combine multiple unrelated sets of data

- combine sets of data with different formats (structured, unstructured, semi-structured)

- process large amounts of data at a time

- filter out data not relevant to the nature of a given analysis

- extract meaningful analysis results from combined data

- identify hidden information from dataset

> **TIP**
> The automated process of sifting through large datasets to identify patterns and trends is referred to as *data mining*.

In addition to supporting decision makers, the data intelligence produced by big data systems can be used to enhance the customer-centricity of digital transformation solutions (Figure 11.3).

The Five V's of Big Data

Data processed by big data systems is distinguished by five characteristics, commonly referred to as the "Five V's" (Figure 11.4):

- *Data Volume* – The anticipated volume of data that is processed by big data systems is substantial and usually ever-growing.

- *Data Velocity* – Data may need to be received and processed at fast speeds that result in the accumulation of large datasets within very short periods of time.

- *Data Variety* – Multiple formats and types of data need to be combined, processed and analyzed.

- *Data Veracity* – This is a measure of "noisy" data that adds no value and can clutter datasets. Big data systems aim for high data veracity by filtering out such data.

- *Data Value* – The extent to which data is useful to an organization.

The value of data can be related to its veracity, but may also be dependent on how long data processing takes. The longer it takes for data to be turned into meaningful information, the less value it may have for the business, because it inhibits the speed at which it can make informed decisions.

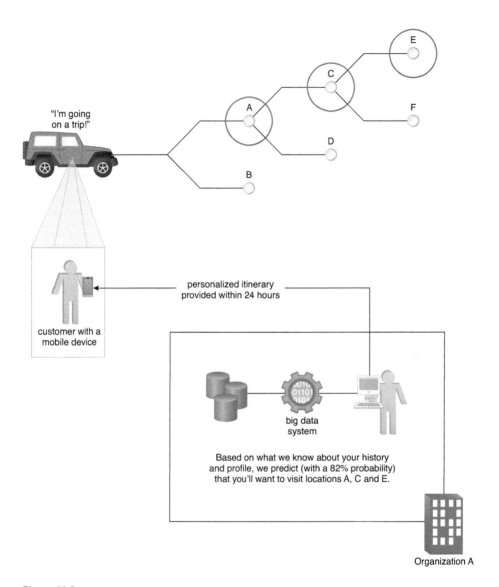

Figure 11.3

A customer would like to go on a sightseeing trip in a new region that the customer never traveled to before. The customer does not want to waste time researching the area and does not want to take a chance on visiting places that may not be interesting. Organization A is hired to provide the customer with a personalized travel itinerary. After issuing the request, the customer is provided with the itinerary the next day. The customer uses the personalized itinerary to visit the recommended locations.

Figure 11.4
The Five V's of big data.

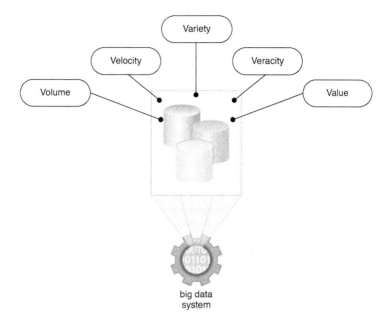

big data
system

Apart from veracity and time, value is also determined by the following considerations:

- How well has the data been filtered?
- How well has the data been stored?
- Were the correct questions being asked during data analysis?
- Were the data analysis results accurately communicated to decision makers?

Big Data in Practice

There are numerous data analytics and analysis techniques that can be used with and are enabled by big data systems. The reporting results are usually provided to decision makers via a dashboard (Figure 11.5) from where they can be assessed and used as input for manual intelligent decision-making.

> **TIP**
> Data visualization tools are used to provide dynamic, interactive dashboards that can be used by humans (without technical skills) to customize data views, such as summarizing data or showing detailed data breakdowns.

Big data practices and systems establish a foundational layer of contemporary data science capabilities for organizations. The sheer amount of disparate data that may need to be collected and processed by an organization undergoing a digital transformation can make it unrealistic to rely solely on manual analysis with big data systems. Furthermore, the

potential need for data to be analyzed in realtime and looped back into digital transformation solutions for on-going processing and automated decisioning functions can
introduce requirements beyond the capabilities of out-of-the-box big data systems. As a
result, big data practices and systems are usually complemented by and extended using
machine learning and AI.

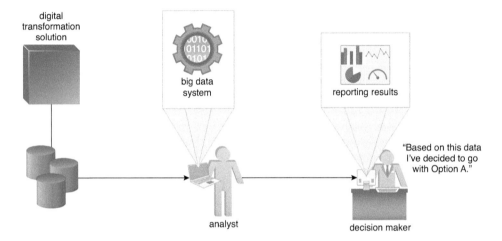

Figure 11.5
A big data system is used to extract meaningful reporting results from a large quantity of diverse data sources. A decision
maker reviews the results via a dashboard and correspondingly makes a decision.

Common Risks and Challenges

- *Data Privacy Concerns* – Performing analytics on datasets can reveal confidential
  information about organizations or individuals. Even analyzing separate datasets
  that contain seemingly anonymous data can reveal private information when the
  datasets are analyzed jointly. This can lead to inadvertent breaches of privacy.

- *Weak Security* – Some big data systems lack the robustness of traditional enterprise
  solution environments when it comes to access control and data security. Secur-
  ing datasets in these environments can require extra attention to ensure that all
  networks and repositories involved have proper security controls in place.

- *Limited Realtime Support* – Dashboards and other parts of big data systems that
  need streaming data and alerts often require realtime or near-realtime data transmissions. Many big data systems and tools are batch-oriented, meaning support
  for streaming data analysis results may either be limited or non-existent.

- *Distinct Performance Challenges* – Due to the volume of data that some big data systems are required to process, performance can sometimes become a concern. For example, large datasets coupled with complex search algorithms can lead to long query times. Another factor can be available bandwidth. With increasing data volume, the time to transfer a given dataset could exceed its actual data processing duration.

Machine Learning

Machine learning systems rely on powerful technology to carry out sophisticated and complex data analysis and analytics. Using machine learning technology, data processing can be carried out rapidly and can often produce results instantly.

A machine learning system is further capable of "learning" from historical training data and the outcome of its data analysis results, leading to opportunities for it to continually improve the quality of the data intelligence it can produce. This enables organizations to gain greater value from data intelligence within a shorter amount of time (Figure 11.6).

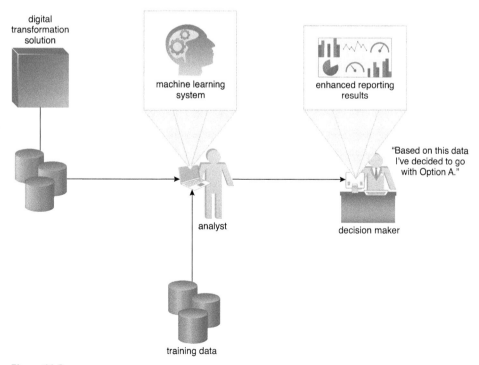

Figure 11.6
An analyst uses a machine learning system to produce enhanced reporting results for a decision maker.

Model Training

The self-learning that a machine learning system can carry out is accomplished with the use of intelligent programs (referred to as *algorithms*) that help shape the logic behind different machine learning approaches (referred to as *models*).

CAUTION
There are many different algorithms you can choose from. Matching the most suitable algorithm to address the unique requirements of the business analysis you want to carry out is a critical success factor when using machine learning.

Once an analyst identifies the analysis requirements for a given problem, an algorithm and model are chosen. The algorithm is used to expose the model to historical training data relevant to the analysis. Iterations of this exposure enable the model to learn about the nature of the data, thereby optimizing it in support of providing a solution to the analysis problem. Once the model has been sufficiently trained, it can be deployed and used to solve the analysis problem with new data as its input (Figure 11.7). Thereafter, the model can be retrained on a regular basis to continue to improve.

There are many types of analysis that can be performed using machine learning. One that is particularly relevant to building customer-centric solutions is the ability to analyze and predict customer behavior. This is accomplished by reviewing and analyzing historical customer data already collected or acquired.

A classic example is when online retailers customize the shopping experience of specific customers by first displaying the products they are most likely to be interested in, based on their purchase history and other factors (Figure 11.8).

Machine Learning in Practice

Machine learning systems can predict customer behavior by analyzing a variety of factors, including:

- prior decisions made by the customer
- geographical movement of the customer
- demographic data associated with the customer's profile
- past behavior of the customer

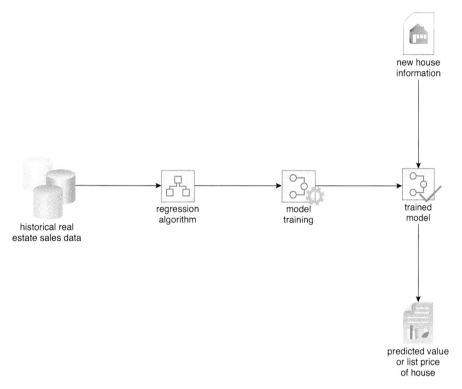

Figure 11.7
A real estate agency uses historical sales data with a trained model to determine the recommended value or listing price for a new house it will be putting up for sale.

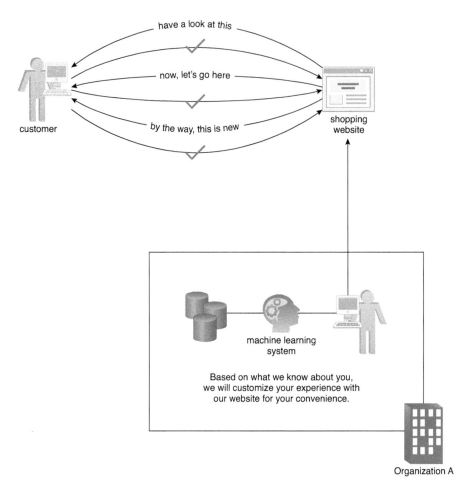

Figure 11.8

A machine learning system is used to improve a customer's shopping experience by customizing the product information being displayed.

These predictions are not limited to customers performing the same actions they previously performed. By analyzing historical data, customer profile data and data from other customers with compatible profiles, a machine learning system can predict the probability of a customer behaving a certain way or having certain interests under new circumstances (Figure 11.9).

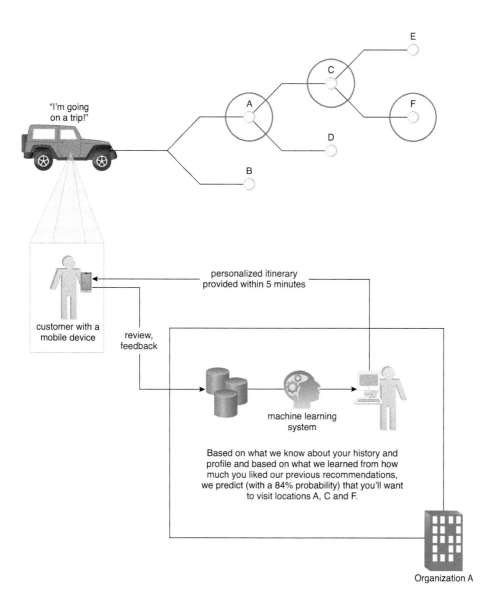

Figure 11.9

The customer requests a personalized travel itinerary, which Organization A generates within a few minutes. Upon completing the trip, the customer provides a review (perhaps with a rating) and feedback to indicate how good the trip was. The machine learning system learns from the feedback and attempts to improve the quality of the next itinerary it provides to this customer. The feedback is also used to contribute to data intelligence used for other types of analysis and in support of other customers.

Depending on the nature of the digital transformation solution logic, several more of analysis practices may be utilized, such as techniques that produce data intelligence that can be used to improve the internal operations of an organization (Figure 11.10).

Common Risks and Challenges

- *Data Volume Requirements* – For machine learning tools to produce effective results, a certain volume of data is required to train models and test the accuracy of algorithms. Therefore, when an insufficient quantity of data is used for training, the system may not be able to identify all of the possible patterns and relationships in the data. This can result in poor or inaccurate predictions or classifications.

- *Data Privacy Restrictions* – Some organizations may struggle with internal and regulatory data privacy requirements that may limit the quantity of available training data. This can limit the effectiveness of machine learning as the tools may not be able to properly train the models.

- *Learning Curve* – Machine learning systems use advanced algorithms. There are many different types of algorithms available from different sources and developed at different times. It can be challenging to navigate through and learn these algorithms in order to effectively choose the one most suited for a given business problem.

- *Quality Assurance* – Quality assurance professionals may often face difficulties when it comes to testing machine learning systems as traditional practices are not generally applicable. Assessing the quality and relevance of the data in particular can be challenging and requires specialized expertise.

> **CAUTION**
> As explained in the *Poor Data Quality and Data Bias* section in Chapter 5, another on-going concern is the processing of poor data or data with bias. If the flaws within data being used for model training purposes go undetected, then the machine learning system can consequently produce data intelligence with flaws that may go undetected for long periods of time.

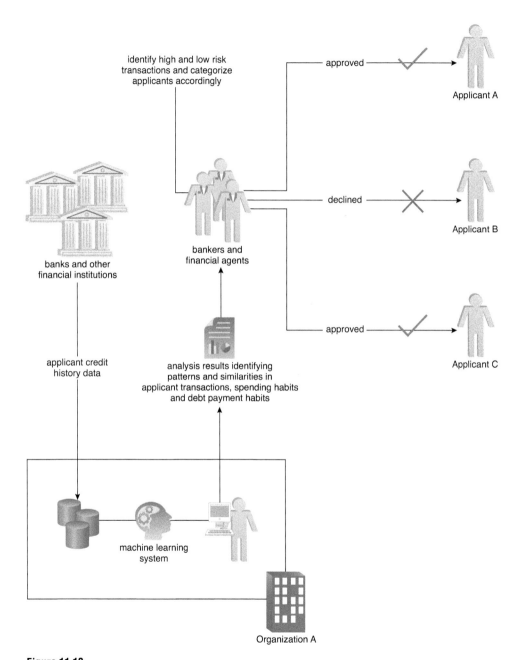

Figure 11.10

When a customer applies for credit with a financial institution, the customer's historical online transaction data is analyzed together with other provided credit information. This data is collectively used to assess risk which helps determine whether the application should be approved or declined. For those applicants approved, the data may further be used to determine the amount of credit that can be extended.

Artificial Intelligence (AI)

When a human attempts to solve a problem or make a decision, the human brain searches through stored information to reference relevant memories that provide input into the problem solving or decision-making process. This concept is known as the *cybernetic loop*, which is the primary inspiration behind artificial intelligence (Figure 11.11).

Figure 11.11
The human brain learns from memory.

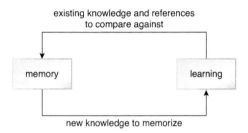

Artificial intelligence (AI) is the field of study dedicated to enabling computers to emulate the functionality of the human brain. This includes the ability to learn, reason and solve problems.

Similar to machine learning, AI systems use algorithms to expose models to historical training data relevant to the analysis objectives. Unlike machine learning, AI systems commonly utilize neural networks as their models.

Neural Networks

A neural network is comprised of functions and different types of neurons (Figure 11.12). By connecting multiple artificial neural cells a neural network is formed, capable of learning from input data to perform sophisticated and complex processing tasks (Figure 11.13).

Figure 11.12
A neuron receives input data, processes it according to its functions and then outputs data to all of that neuron's connected neurons

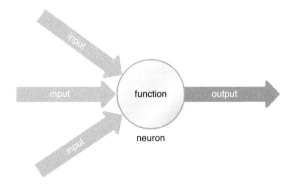

Figure 11.13

An example of an artificial neural network. In different types of neural network architectures, it is common for there to be different numbers of hidden layers and different numbers of neurons in the hidden layers, depending on the complexity of the information processing requirements.

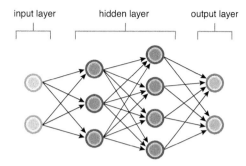

Using neural networks, AI systems can:

- identify rules, patterns, commonalities and formulate predictions

- reason to derive logical outcomes

- classify and extract data

- provide input for decision-making

Automated Decision-Making

AI systems further have the ability to carry out decisions autonomously. This is the basis of the automated decision-making models covered in *Chapter 8: Intelligent Decision-Making*. In addition to being able to learn from the outcome of analysis results, an AI system can learn from the outcome of its decisions to help improve how it makes decisions in the future (Figure 11.14).

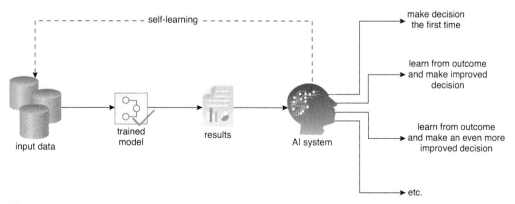

Figure 11.14

The AI system can repeatedly look up and analyze previously input data in order to learn from prior outcomes so that it can improve future outcomes.

Automated decision-making can be positioned within customer-centric solutions in many different ways to both improve the efficiency of an organization's operations, as well as its responsiveness to the customers themselves (Figure 11.15).

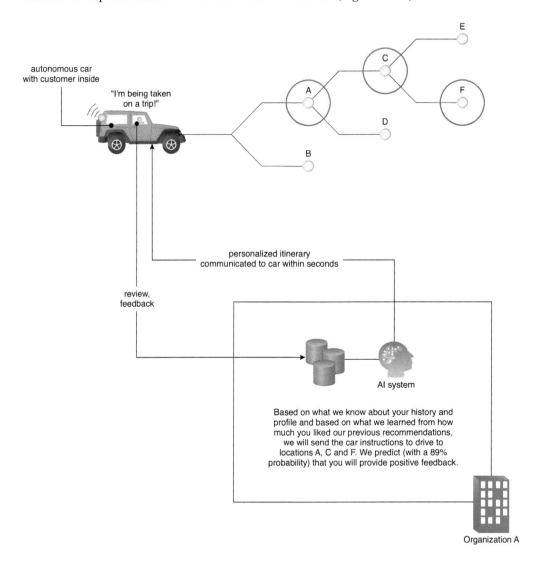

Figure 11.15

AI system logic is used by a car to drive a customer autonomously to a series of sight seeing destinations that are also determined by the AI system based on its knowledge of the customer's profile, history, predicted interests and feedback from which it learns to improve both analysis results (destinations) and decision-making. (The autonomous car is equipped with an IoT sensor and is colored blue because it is now an active extension of the digital transformation solution.)

AI in Practice

AI systems can be utilized to enable customer-centricity in many other ways, including:

- *Complex Analysis* – Applying complex information processing to large, diverse datasets in order to gain deep business insights into individual customer profiles, customer trends and customer sentiment.

- *Graphical Recognition* – Recognizing handwriting, faces and objects in images and tracking recognized objects on motion video to improve customer-centric solutions that require this type of functionality and to further improve realtime customer interactions.

- *Language and Sentiment Analysis* – Recognizing, interpreting and responding in human languages (including sentiment and emotional content) to help foster warm customer interactions.

AI systems can generate (realtime or near-realtime) prediction and forecasting analysis results in support of both manual and automated intelligent decision-making (Figure 11.16).

Common Risks and Challenges

- *Learning Curve and Incomprehensible Decision-Making* – AI systems can be highly complex, both in terms of their design as well as complexity in working with the data intelligence they create. For example, a data analyst may not always fully understand or be able to justify the rationale behind the decisions that an AI system makes. This can occur when those responsible for implementing and working with the AI system do not have a sufficiently deep level of understanding of the underlying algorithms and logic that the system is using. It can also occur when the AI system is using faulty data or has not been correctly designed or configured. It is important that analysts and others that work with AI systems have a deep enough understanding of its inner workings to know, with certainty, that decisions being made by the AI system are correct and justifiable.

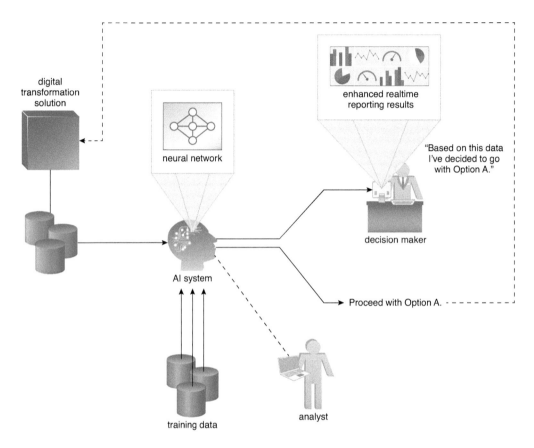

Figure 11.16

An AI system with a neural network produces enhanced realtime reporting results for a human decision maker, while using those results to also carry out automated decision-making.

- *Distrust by Humans* – In some industries, AI has a reputation of being a form of technology that leads to increased unemployment rates. This is because AI systems have the potential of superseding human decision makers, as well as other human workers (such as when coupled with RPA to carry out intelligent automation). AI systems can further be designed to emulate human behavior, which can lead to other opportunities to supersede human workers. While AI systems can enable the intelligent automation of many manual tasks, they can also introduce opportunities for new innovative products and technologies that result in business growth that can lead to new jobs. Either way, concerns about AI systems replacing humans can lead to hesitance and resistance when it comes to AI technology adoption.

- *Data Hosting and Access Restrictions* – In order to remain responsive and adaptive, AI systems can demand very large amounts of data continuously fed to them for ongoing processing tasks. There can be practical challenges associated with providing such data, especially when relying on cloud-based environments for the data's hosting and processing. Data privacy policies and regulations may make it difficult or impossible to use cloud environments or preferred data centers, which can void the benefit of being able to leverage inexpensive infrastructure for storage and high-performance computing. In other cases, the volume of required data may simply not be available, or the quality of available data may be insufficient.

- *Quality Assurance* – It can be challenging to subject an AI system to quality assurance practices when its output and overall behavior cannot always be predetermined or predicted. Self-learning logic can lead to new outcomes that may not have been anticipated by the AI system owners. Furthermore, AI systems are potentially capable of self-learning beyond their initial functional scope. This means that an AI system can possibly broaden its knowledge autonomously, like a human. These characteristics of AI systems can make them difficult to assess and measure from a QA perspective.

CAUTION
The same concerns regarding data bias and poor data quality raised in the previous sections in this chapter also apply to AI, only these concerns are amplified when an AI system is at risk of using flawed data to carry out automated decision-making tasks.

Chapter 12

Inside a Customer-Centric Solution

In this final chapter we get to experience digital transformation in action. We will be going on a customer-centric journey while taking a look under the hood to understand, each step of the way, what a digital transformation solution is doing. We will see how the solution uses data intelligence to improve the customer journey, while also continually collecting new data to enhance the existing data intelligence. So, buckle up and let's go!

The chapters in the book so far have covered a range of topics that explain and relate to the technology and practices behind digital transformation and the realization of customer-centricity. This final chapter provides an exploration of a customer journey as enabled by digital transformation technology and a customer-centric business process.

The purpose of this chapter is to:

- demonstrate the practices of customer-centricity

- indicate how and where digital transformation technology can be utilized to improve a customer journey

- highlight how the utilization of customer-centricity practices and digital transformation technology can realize strategic business objectives

The chapter begins by establishing some background information about a car manufacturing company and its car purchasing business process. The pre-digital transformation workflow is described, along with the business objectives the company used as the basis of its digital transformation.

Before the chapter moves on to describe the new customer-centric business process and its automation solution, a recap of key terms is provided. These are terms associated with important topics covered in Chapters 6 to 11. To best link these topics to the coverage of the digital transformation solution, the associated terms are colored blue throughout the remainder of this chapter.

The chapter then dives into a step-by-step exploration of the car purchasing customer journey. With each step, the involvement of any one of the seven primary digital transformation automation and data science technologies is highlighted, along with an explanation of how these technologies are utilized behind the scenes.

Scenario Background

A car manufacturing company has been undergoing an organization-wide digital transformation. One of its primary goals was to transform its existing car purchasing business process for which it identified challenges and deficiencies and corresponding objectives and improvements.

Business Challenges

The car manufacturing company had accumulated a significant amount of information that indicated inadequacies in how the car purchasing process was being carried out and in how customers experienced it.

These issues included:

- A sales conversion rate that was below the industry average. In other words, customers visiting dealerships were not purchasing cars as frequently as at dealerships from competing car manufacturers.

- Mediocre feedback from customer satisfaction surveys submitted by customers that have purchased cars.

- Poor feedback from dealership sales staff that indicated that they were not given sufficient information or tools to improve car sales and customer satisfaction.

- A below average car service rate, meaning that after a customer purchased a car, there was only a fair probability the customer would return to the dealership for service.

There was also a low repeat business rate. Historically, customers that purchased cars from a dealership were not likely to purchase their next cars from the same dealership.

Upon a review of all available information, the car manufacturer determined that there was a strong likelihood that the low level of customer loyalty was related to the inadequacies of the car purchasing customer journey and the lack of effort dealerships made to stay connected with customers after cars were sold.

The next section provides a brief overview of the original car purchasing business process.

The Original Customer Journey

The car purchasing business process was originally product-centric, whereby the dealership carried out only the most necessary steps associated with selling a car and providing the ordered car to the customer.

Figure 12.1 illustrates the primary steps in the business process. These steps are described thereafter and then further organized into a workflow in Figure 12.1.

The individual steps are briefly explained here:

1. *Customer Visits Dealership* – A customer visits a car dealership to browse available cars for sale.

2. *Customer Makes Inquiry* – The customer inquires about a specific car by talking to a sales person. Historically, there is a less-than-average probability that the customer will further explore purchasing this car after receiving more information about it from the sales person.

3. *Options Shown to Customer* – If the customer does want to learn more about the car, the sales person shows the customer available options and packages for the model of the car.

4. *Price Shown to Customer* – Based on the option chosen by the customer, the sales person shows the price of the car and informs the customer it will be delivered in 4–6 weeks.

5. *Customer Places Order?*

6. *Customer Leaves* – If the customer does not place the order for the car, the customer leaves the dealership.

7. *Dealership Processes Order* – If the customer does place the order for the car, the sales person processes the order.

8. *Dealership Calls for Delivery* – A couple of weeks later, the sales person calls the car manufacturer to find out how much longer it will take for the car to be delivered.

9. *Dealership Calls Customer* – The sales person calls to inform the customer as to when the car will arrive.

10. *Production Scheduling Change?*

11. *Dealership Notifies Customer* – If there is a change in the delivery date of the car due to a production scheduling change with the car manufacturer, the sales person informs the customer by phone.

12. *Manufacturer Ships Car* – When the car is ready, it is shipped by the manufacturer to the dealership.

13. *Dealership Notifies Customer* – Upon arrival of the car, the sales person informs the customer by phone.

14. *Dealership Provides Car* – The customer picks up the new car from the dealership.

15. *Customer Takes Car* – The customer drives away in the new car.

Figure 12.2 provides a workflow view of how these steps are carried out.

Figure 12.1

A customer journey involving interactions with a car dealership over a period of days in order to purchase and deliver a new car. (The numbers in this diagram are those shown in the workflow depicted in Figure 12.2. Not shown is Step 6, which occurs if the customer does not proceed with the purchase of the new car.)

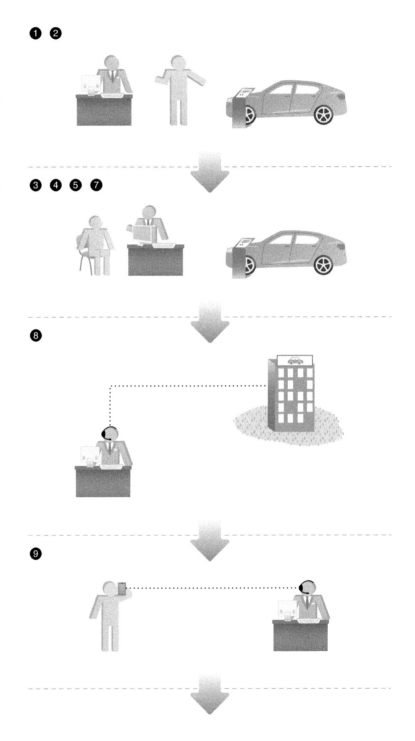

**Figure 12.1
(continued)**

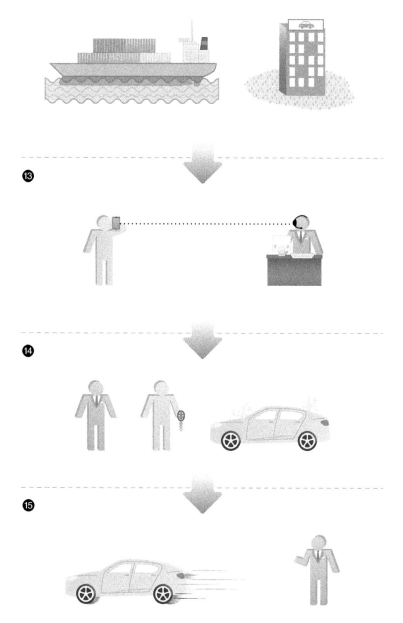

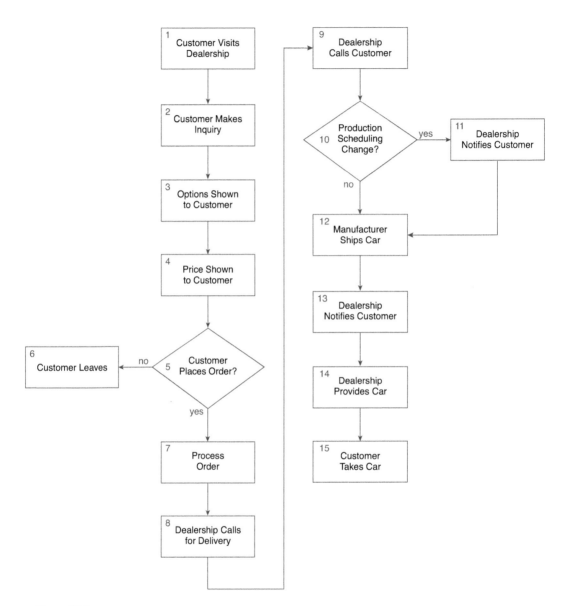

Figure 12.2
The customer journey workflow illustrating the steps described earlier.

Business Objectives

The car manufacturing company identified the following business goals it intended to achieve specifically in relation to the car purchasing business process:

- improve customer satisfaction

- improve customer engagement

- improve customer service efficiency

- increase return business

An additional goal was for the company to merge the car purchasing business process with a separate, less formal process that was being carried out to sell a road-side assistance plan.

Originally, after a car was sold, the dealership would contact the customer a week or two later to offer a road-side assistance plan at a promotional discount. The rate at which this plan was sold was low in that only 1 in 10 customers purchased the plan. The company therefore wanted to leverage digital transformation to merge the business processes of the two products (the car and the plan) into a single business process.

Terminology Recap

The six preceding chapters covered a series of topics pertaining to digital transformation and customer-centricity. The terminology established in these chapters is summarized in this section for reference purposes.

The key terms are organized in Tables 12.1 to 12.6 and are colored blue during the remainder of this chapter to help identify how they relate to the upcoming digital transformation solution and the associated customer journey.

Key Terms from Chapter 6: Realizing Customer-Centricity

Customer Action Types	Customer Warmth Types	Customer Interaction Channel Types
Transaction-Value Action	Communicative Warmth	Single-Channel
Relationship-Value Action	Proactive Warmth	Multi-Channel
Customer-Facing Action	Rewardful Warmth	Omni-Channel
Customer-Oriented Action	Exceeding Warmth	

Table 12.1
These terms are focused on describing and categorizing different types of customer-centricity.

Key Terms from Chapter 7: Data Intelligence Basics

Data Sources	Data Collection Methods	Data Utilization Types
Operations Data	Manual Data Entry	Analysis and Reporting
Customer Data	Automated Data Entry	Solution Input
Social Media Data	Telemetry Data Capture	Automated Decision-Making
Public Sector Data	Digitization	Bot-Driven Automation
Private Sector Data	Data Ingress	Model Training & Retraining
		Historical Record Keeping

Table 12.2
These terms define and classify the sources of data, as well as how the data can be collected and used.

Key Terms from Chapter 8: Intelligent Decision-Making

Decision-Making Types
Manual Decision-Making
Conditional Automated Decision-Making
Intelligent Manual Decision-Making
Intelligent Automated Decision-Making

Intelligent Automated Decision-Making Types
Direct-Driven Automated Decision-Making
Periodic Automated Decision-Making
Realtime Automated Decision-Making

Table 12.3
The basic decision-making types, as well as the automated decision-making types are defined with these key terms.

Key Terms from Chapter 9: Understanding Digital Transformation Solutions

Data Ingress Types
File Pull
File Push
API Pull
API Push
Data Streaming

Table 12.4
The methods by which data is brought into organizations are identified with these terms.

Key Terms from Chapter 10: An Introduction to Digital Transformation Automation Technologies

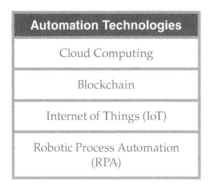

Table 12.5
These terms represent the primary digital transformation automation technologies.

Key Terms from Chapter 11: An Introduction to Digital Transformation Data Science Technologies

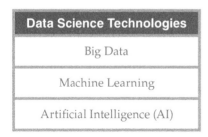

Table 12.6
These terms represent the primary digital transformation data science technologies.

The Enhanced Customer Journey

To achieve the previously described business objectives, business analysts from different parts of the organization collaborated to produce a new, expanded business process that introduced a number of enhancements, including:

- A customer-centric approach, whereby building a mutually beneficial, long-term relationship with the customer is advocated, where applicable.

- A consolidated workflow that encompasses and links the purchase processes of two products, the car and the road-side assistance plan.

- The use of digital transformation automation technologies to optimize the business process and improve its capabilities.

- The use of digital transformation data science technologies to increase the quantity and improve the quality of data intelligence utilized to maximize the probability of a successful outcome of the business process.

- The careful utilization of intelligent automated decision-making to improve the efficiency of the customer journey, without introducing unreasonable risk.

- A structured workflow geared toward collecting meaningful customer data intelligence, regardless of whether product purchases are successful.

Most of the remainder of this chapter is dedicated to providing detailed, step-by-step descriptions of the enhanced customer journey. Prior to exploring this new business process, the supporting data sources are first briefly explained and illustrated.

Supporting Data Sources

- *Customer Data* – The interaction between the customer and the dealership throughout the customer journey results in an accumulation of customer data intelligence used both to support the experience of that customer, and to feed into the pool of customer data collected by the data science systems in support of improving other business processes and in support of their future learning, analysis, reporting and decision-making requirements.

- *Operations Data (from customer)* – In addition to the data collected about the customer, the interactions of the customer with the dealership lead to the creation of new operations data pertaining to products, transactions and other data resulting from business activity. This data is used to complete the business tasks that are part of the car purchasing business process, and is also provided to the underlying data science systems as input for future learning, analysis, reporting and decision-making purposes.

- *Operations Data (from telemetry streams)* – The provisioning steps in the business process result in the generation of operations data comprised of delivery route information, collected via data streaming and telemetry data capture. This data is shared with the customer as a means of improving customer engagement during the customer journey. The data is also stored and fed to the underlying data science systems as input for future learning, analysis, reporting and decision-making purposes.

- *Social Media Data* – The car manufacturer has an on-going subscription with a social media site from which it retrieves weekly datasets via API pull messages. The data it receives is pre-filtered and limited to comments posted about the company's own car models. This data is provided to the underlying data science systems as input for future learning, analysis, reporting and decision-making purposes.

- *Public Sector Data* – The car manufacturer periodically carries out a file pull to retrieve public sector data consisting of the latest statistics published by the local government's Department of Transportation. This data, comprised primarily of traffic, fuel consumption and pollution statistics, is provided to the underlying data science systems as input for future learning, analysis, reporting and decision-making purposes.

- *Private Sector Data* – RPA bots are utilized on-demand to collect data from competitors within the local business community. This data is used as input to help generate attractive product prices for the customer and is also stored for historical reference purposes.

Figure 12.3 illustrates these data sources and further shows the car manufacturer's current data ingress channels.

Step-by-Step Business Process

Figure 12.4 displays a workflow illustration of the new, expanded car purchasing business process. The remainder of this chapter provides individual descriptions of the steps shown in the workflow.

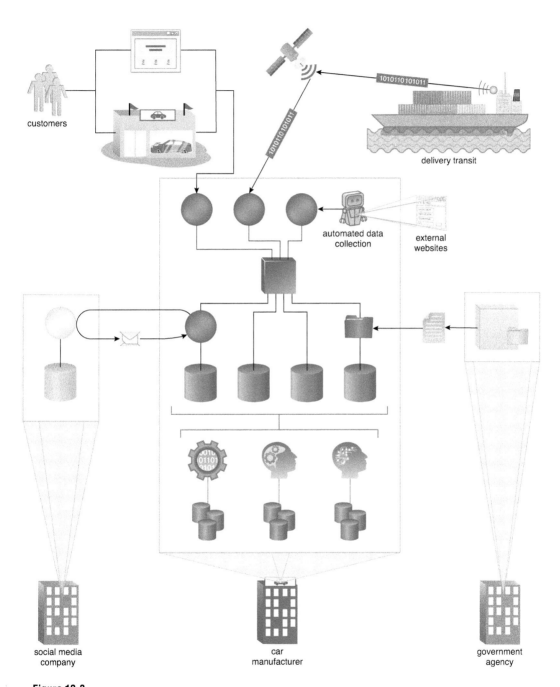

customers

delivery transit

automated data collection

external websites

social media company

car manufacturer

government agency

Figure 12.3

The car manufacturer receives data from different third-party data sources, as well as internally generated corporate data. Big data, machine learning and AI systems are used to process this data to create and improve data intelligence on an on-going basis.

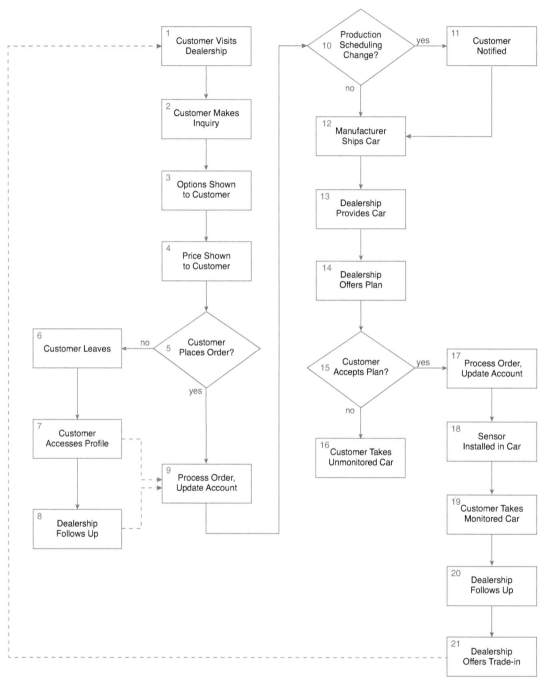

Figure 12.4
The enhanced customer journey as illustrated in a workflow.

Each of the following step descriptions includes:

- an explanation of the customer experience

- an explanation of the back-end processing carried out by the digital transformation solution (when applicable)

The involvement of digital transformation technologies is intentionally kept at an abstract level so as to focus more on where individual technologies are involved, as opposed to the technical details of how they function.

Step 1. Customer Visits Dealership

A customer visits a car dealership to browse available cars for sale (Figure 12.5).

During the customer's visit at the dealership, a sales person (Figure 12.6) will become the customer's point of contact for all customer-facing actions during this customer journey.

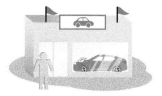

Figure 12.5
The customer journey begins with the customer visiting a car dealership in person.

Figure 12.6
Throughout this customer journey, the sales person will be using a workstation connected to a digital transformation solution to carry out business tasks that are part of the car purchasing process.

Step 2. Customer Makes Inquiry

The customer inquires about a specific car by talking to the sales person. The sales person pulls up a dashboard on a workstation with a wide range of realtime operations data about the specific car model, such as:

- stock levels in different geographical locations

- past sales statistics compared to similar models (from the manufacturer and/or competitors)

- common profile information based on past buyers

- statistics pertaining to typical quantity of annual repairs, safety rating and power consumption

The sales person can even access and share past social media and web reviews provided by buyers or third-party reviewers.

Using the information displayed by the dashboard, the sales person is able to provide a rich amount of insightful information about the specific car model with exceeding warmth, well beyond what the customer was expecting. This, combined with communicative warmth, can impress and engage the customer to increase the probability of the customer exploring the purchase of the car (Figure 12.7).

Figure 12.7

For the sales person to gain instant access to detailed and insightful data relevant to the customer's query, cloud computing and machine learning technologies are utilized on the back end.

Together with the current inventory levels, the sales person is also immediately able to view the upcoming production schedule of the specific car model. If inventory levels are sparse or if no further cars are scheduled for production (such as when the car model will be superseded by another), the sales person can inform the customer that the car may be difficult to acquire and, using additional operations data, keep the customer engaged by suggesting and providing details about alternative models.

The dashboard interacts with a digital transformation solution that includes a cloud-hosted service and a machine learning system that generates a dynamic report comprised of a range of data about the car model being discussed. This data is presented on-demand back to the sales person's workstation dashboard (Figure 12.8).

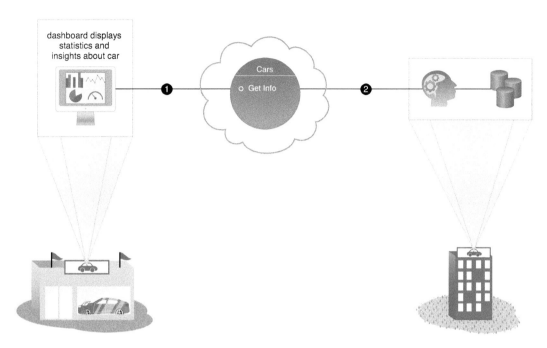

Figure 12.8

The sales person's workstation issues a request for the most current data available about the car that the customer inquired about. The request invokes the cloud-based Cars service (1), which interacts with the organization's IT back end, including a machine learning system, to retrieve the most current requested data on-demand (2).

Step 3. Options Shown to Customer

The customer sits down with the sales person to learn more about the customization options available for the car model. These options can include different individual features and add-ons (such as special wheels, paint colors, sound systems, etc.), as well as packages that provide bundled features and add-ons.

There is a set of pre-defined options that the sales person can show. However, there is also the opportunity to generate custom packages of features and add-ons more tailored to the customer.

As part of this step (and to lay a foundation for the dealership to carry out future relationship-value actions), the sales person first attempts to collect some basic customer data in order to better understand the customer's overall interests and preferences as they may relate to the car—and—with the customer's consent, to set up a preliminary customer profile account in the digital transformation solution.

Using the customer profile data as input, the sales person then issues a request for the options (Figure 12.9).

Figure 12.9
For the sales person to receive customized options for the car, cloud computing and machine learning technologies are used on the back end.

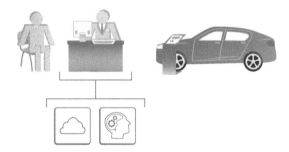

The sales person uses the workstation to carry out the manual data entry of customer data. The workstation communicates with a digital transformation solution that includes cloud-hosted services and a machine learning system that receives both customer data and operations data about the car. It uses this data as input to generate the requested data that is then displayed on the sales person's workstation (Figure 12.10).

The results may include only customized options or a combination of pre-defined and customized options. The results may also only include pre-defined options if insufficient customer profile data was received.

NOTE
Ultimately, the decision maker in this step is the customer. The options are presented to enable the customer to carry out intelligent manual decision-making.

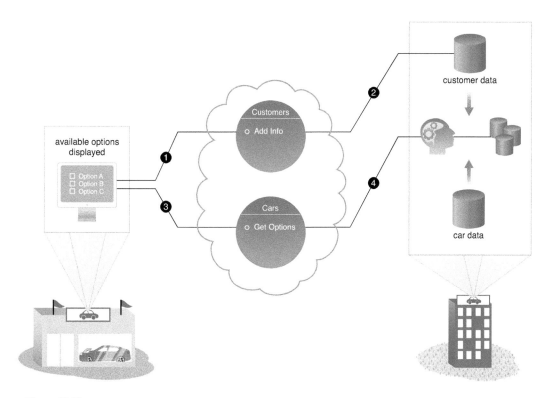

Figure 12.10

The sales person's workstation first collects relevant customer profile data and then invokes the Customers service (1), which accesses the organization's IT back end to create a new customer profile (if one did not previously exist) in which to record the new customer data (2). When the sales person then issues the request for the options, the workstation invokes the Cars service (3), which interacts with the IT back end that includes a machine learning system (4) that factors in available customer data and operations data to generate the requested analysis and reporting options. The solution could also subsequently record the level of interest the customer expresses in the presented options (not shown) to assist the machine learning system with future learning and analysis.

Step 4. Price Shown to Customer

Once the customer has chosen an option, the sales person prepares to present the price. Because this is a pivotal step in the customer journey, it involves a number of back-end technologies that work together to carry out a series of customer-oriented actions in order to determine and propose a price that is attractive and has a high probability of being acceptable to the customer.

The sales person begins by asking the customer for more information, such as payment preferences (cash, financing, leasing, etc.), whether the customer has a car to trade in and how much of a down payment the customer may be able to provide. This customer data is also added to the customer profile. The sales person then issues a request for the price (Figure 12.11).

Figure 12.11

Based on the customer profile data collected so far and based on the current local marketplace for this specific car model, the sales person wants to present the most attractive price possible to the customer. To accomplish this, cloud computing, RPA and AI technologies are used on the back end.

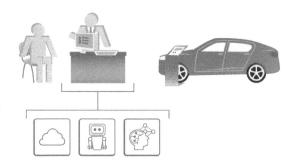

Using the workstation, the sales person updates the customer's profile with the newly collected data. Upon then requesting the price, the workstation communicates with the digital transformation solution, which utilizes RPA and cloud computing technologies, together with an AI system, to carry out direct-driven automated decision-making to generate a price custom-tailored for the customer (Figure 12.12).

The factors taken into account when determining this price include:

- local market information about prices of comparable cars from competing dealerships in the vicinity (private sector data)

- the standard pricing used for the car (operations data)

- additional information collected about the customer's payment preferences (customer data)

The digital transformation solution factors in these considerations in realtime each time a price is requested. This means that the presented price can vary with each request, unless additional logic is added to limit the extent to which prices can fluctuate during a given period of time.

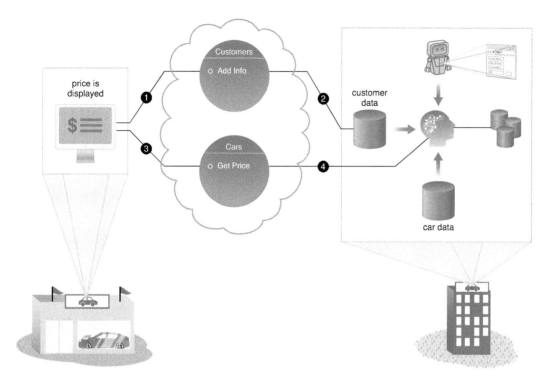

Figure 12.12
The sales person updates the customer profile with the additional customer data collected. The workstation invokes the Customers service (1), which accesses the IT back end to update the customer profile record (2). When the sales person is ready to present the price to the customer, the request for the price is submitted to the Cars service (3), which triggers a series of steps on the IT back end (4). First, bot-driven automation is carried out, whereby an RPA bot performs automated data collection by carrying out online searches of websites belonging to competing dealerships in the geographical vicinity of the dealership being visited by the customer. The searches focus on display prices and promotions of comparable car models. The collected private sector data is made available to an AI system that also factors in customer data from the customer profile, as well as the standard car pricing operations data, before deciding on the price amount to present to the customer. This range of input data is sufficient for the AI system to perform the direct-driven automated decision-making required to generate the proposed price.

Step 5. Customer Places Order?

If the customer decides not to place the order, proceed to Steps 6, 7 and 8.

If the customer does place the order, proceed to Step 9.

Step 6. Customer Leaves

After reviewing the price, the customer decides not to proceed with the purchase of the car. Before the customer leaves, the sales person asks the customer for permission to set up a mobile app on the customer's mobile device.

This app will enable the customer to retain access to the car design based on the feature and add-on options explored so far, and will also give the customer access to a subset of the customer profile data. The sales person explains that with this app, the customer will be able to further experiment with other car design options at any time.

The sales person then retains communicative warmth to ensure that the customer leaves with a positive attitude. Upon the customer leaving, the sales person updates the customer data in the profile to indicate that the sale did not proceed (Figure 12.13).

Figure 12.13
The customer leaves and the presentation of the price to the customer is considered to have not succeeded. Using technologies, including cloud computing, this information is provided to the AI system to learn from.

Upon confirming that the customer is not proceeding with the purchase of the car, the sales person updates the customer profile with a "rejected" status associated with the proposed price. This is recorded within the digital transformation solution and this data may also then be used for model retraining purposes for the AI system to improve its future decision-making capability when it comes to deciding on prices to present to customers (Figure 12.14).

The AI system will further use this input to determine the best time to follow up with the customer, as per Step 7.

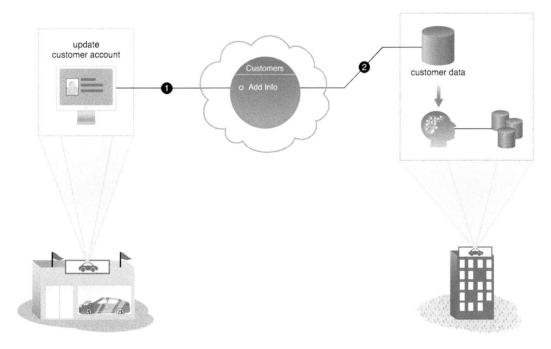

Figure 12.14
The sales person's workstation sends the updated information to the Customers service (1), which relays it to the IT back end where it makes its way into the customer database (2). During the next export of customer data to be analyzed, the AI system learns of the customer rejecting the price it decided to offer. This may be used for model retraining purposes to improve the AI system's overall pricing logic and as a starting point for an eventual follow-up interaction with that customer.

Step 7. Customer Accesses Profile

After leaving the dealership, the customer may use the mobile app to access the car design that was last set up by the sales person in Step 6. The customer can then further explore different add-ons and features that will correspondingly display different prices. This may lead the customer to return to the dealership to proceed with the order (Figure 12.15).

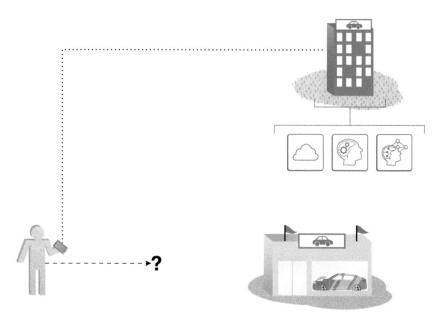

Figure 12.15

The remote access to the online mobile app allows the customer to continue to remain engaged with the car purchasing process. This step involves cloud computing, machine learning and AI technologies.

The customer uses the mobile app to access the customer profile and car design (Figure 12.16). Only a subset of available customer data is presented in the mobile app. For example, the app may only provide access to contact information to enable the customer to update contact details if they should change.

The IT back end logs each of the customer's activities with the mobile app, including the different car design options the customer may try out. The digital transformation solution provides omni-channel support that then enables the dealership to retrieve the customer's most current design and preferences during any subsequent interaction with the customer.

Furthermore, the frequency and extent to which the customer uses the mobile app's car design options may further be factored into how the AI system decides to carry out Step 8.

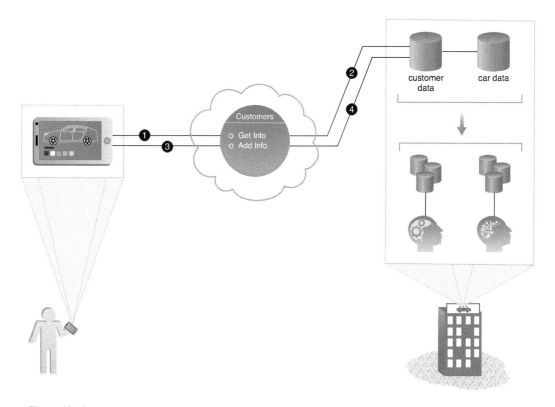

Figure 12.16

When the customer uses the mobile app, it invokes the Customers service (1), which accesses the back end to retrieve select customer data and the associated car design (2). Upon updating the car design options, the app invokes the Customers service again (3) to add the new customer profile data on the back end (4). The updated customer data is also made available to machine learning and AI systems as new input that these systems can use for future model training, analysis and reporting, and automated decision-making purposes.

Step 8. Dealership Follows Up

Over the next few days, the car manufacturer periodically carries out customer-oriented actions to check to see if a better price can be made available for the car that the customer inquired about.

If the back-end customer data indicates that the customer has been using the mobile app to explore car options, the car manufacturer will gain an understanding of the customer's on-going interest level. When it becomes clear that the customer has settled on a new design option, the focus will turn to finding an attractive price for that new option.

Once a suitable price is found, the sales person is asked to carry out proactive warmth by reaching out to inform the customer about a new, better price for the car (Figure 12.17). Or, perhaps, to suggest alternative options based on the customer's expressed interests and preferences.

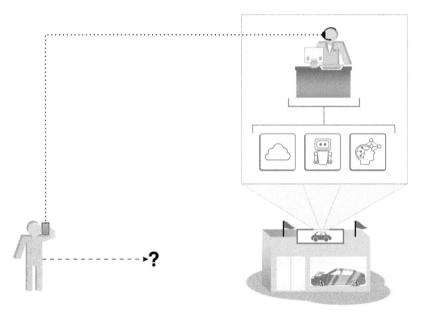

Figure 12.17
The organization's IT back end, driven by the AI system, decides to generate a new, more competitive price. Other technologies involved in this step are cloud computing and RPA.

The AI system performs periodic automated decision-making whereby it directs the digital transformation solution to iterate the process of bot-driven automation by having the RPA bot perform fresh website searches that are then processed by the AI system together with other input data. This iteration occurs until the AI system determines that the conditions are suitable for it to generate a new, more competitive price.

When it reaches that point, it carries out realtime automated decision-making by deciding that it's time for the dealership to communicate the new price to the customer (Figure 12.18). The frequency with which the customer has used or is using the mobile app may further influence when the AI system may decide to communicate a new price. For example, if the customer is actively experimenting with different design options, the AI system may hold off until it appears that the customer has settled on a particular option.

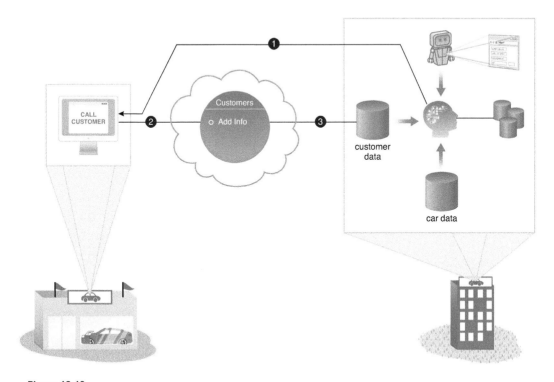

Figure 12.18
After a number of iterations whereby the RPA bot searches for the latest competitive pricing information, the AI system
decides it is time for the sales person to contact the customer and propose a new price (1). The sales person communicates
the new price to the customer and then records the response in the customer profile, for which the customer data is updated
on the back end via the Customers service (2, 3).

If the customer is agreeable to the new price being presented, the process proceeds to
Step 9. If the customer still does not want to purchase the car, the customer data in the
profile is updated correspondingly and the AI system may further receive this data for
model retraining purposes.

Step 9. Process Order and Update Customer Account

Subsequent to reviewing the price, the customer decides to proceed with the purchase
of the car. The sales person collects all the customer data necessary to:

- complete the set up of the customer profile account
- collect the payment information

- process the order for the car

- process the payment for a deposit

After successfully completing these steps, the customer is given a delivery date for the new car. The sales person points out that the delivery date may be subject to change. The customer is assured that there will be automatic notifications of any changes to the delivery schedule and that the customer will also be notified as soon as the car arrives (Figure 12.19). The customer then leaves, and the car manufacturing process is underway.

Figure 12.19
The sales person collects more customer data and processes the order for the new car. On the back end, this involves cloud computing, blockchain, machine learning and AI technologies.

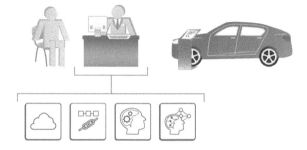

NOTE
How these individual tasks are carried out can vary, depending on whether the customer is paying cash or applying for financing, and also on whether the customer is purchasing or leasing the car. Some of these options would introduce additional steps and tasks not shown in this section.

The sales person uses the workstation to update the customer's profile and submit the order for the car with the feature and add-on options chosen by the customer. This updates both customer data and order data (operations data) stored at the organization's IT back end. Order payment data is further stored in an immutable blockchain repository where it will remain to support future auditing and historical record keeping requirements (Figure 12.20).

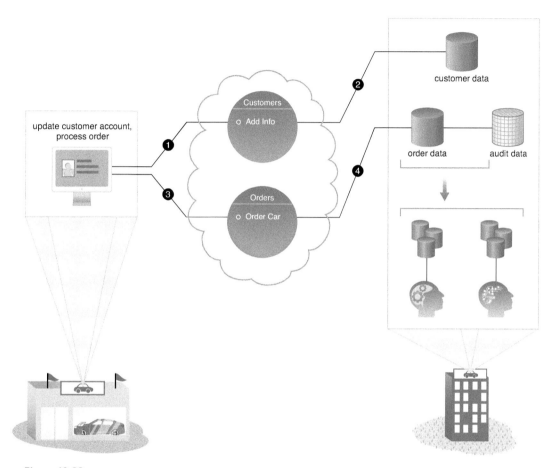

Figure 12.20

The updates to the customer data are made via the Customers service (1), which accesses the IT back end to update the customer profile record (2). The sales person then processes the order for the car model the customer chose, including any selected features and add-ons. This invokes the Orders service (3) that updates operations data by registering the order on the IT back end and further carries out a partial business data capture so that select order and payment data are redundantly stored in the blockchain repository (4). The new customer and order data are made available to machine learning and AI systems as new input that these systems can use for future model training, analysis and reporting, and automated decision-making purposes.

> **NOTE**
>
> The submission of an order for a new car will kick off a new business process within the car manufacturer's office dedicated to all of the manual and automated tasks and logistics required to assemble, customize and deliver the new car back to the dealership. These steps are not covered in this scenario. The next step in this workflow skips ahead to when the car is being manufactured.

Step 10. Production Scheduling Change?

If the car manufacturer needs to change the delivery date of the car, proceed to Step 11.

If the car manufacturer does not need to change the delivery date of the car, proceed to Step 12.

Step 11. Customer is Notified

The car manufacturer needs to change the original delivery date. The car manufacturer updates the customer data within the customer profile with the new estimated delivery date and then determines how to notify the customer (Figure 12.21).

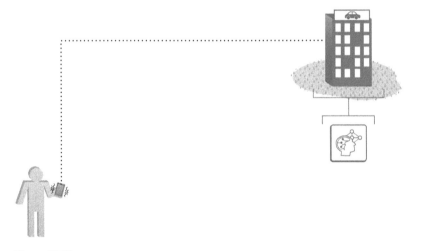

Figure 12.21
The customer may be notified via text or email of a change in the delivery schedule, as directed by the back-end AI system.

There are several possible notification scenarios. The AI system on the back end carries out realtime automated decision-making to determine how, when or whether to notify the customer of the change in the delivery date (Figure 12.22).

It may factor in several considerations when making this decision, such as:

• If the new delivery date may still be subject to further change, it may hold off the notification for a certain period of time until it is fully confirmed.

• If the change in the delivery date is minor (such as a few days), the AI system may determine that notification via a simple text message or email is sufficient.

- If the change in the delivery the date is significant (such as several weeks), the AI system may determine that the sales person should call the customer in person to convey the new delivery date with communicative warmth.

There may be additional data in the customer profile that may help the AI system decide on a more specific course of action. For example, if the customer had previously expressed dissatisfaction during the customer journey so far, the AI system may decide that the sales person should still contact the customer in person with communicative warmth (or perhaps even rewardful warmth), even if the delivery date change is minor.

> **NOTE**
>
> The AI system may be further configured to issue notifications that simply add an element of communicative warmth by providing reassurance that the original delivery schedule is still confirmed, especially during longer wait times.

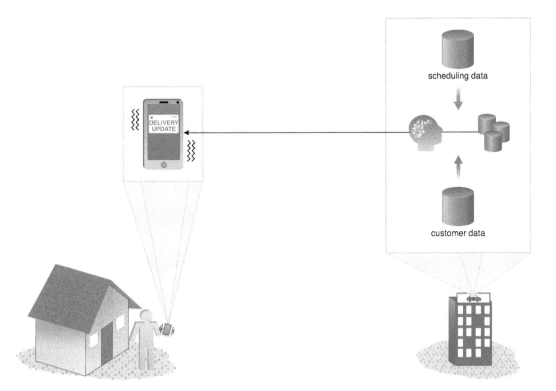

Figure 12.22
Upon a change to the scheduling data, the AI system determines that it is best to notify the customer via a text message.

Step 12. Manufacturer Ships Car

After the car is assembled and ready to go, it is loaded on a cargo boat to be shipped to the dealership. The car manufacturer attaches a sensor device to the car. This device is capable of transmitting its GPS location. This allows the car manufacturer to always determine the location of the car once it is underway.

To increase the excitement for the customer waiting to receive the ordered vehicle during the final stage of delivery, the car manufacturer demonstrates exceeding warmth by providing the ability for the customer (and the dealership) to visually track the car location while in transit (Figure 12.23).

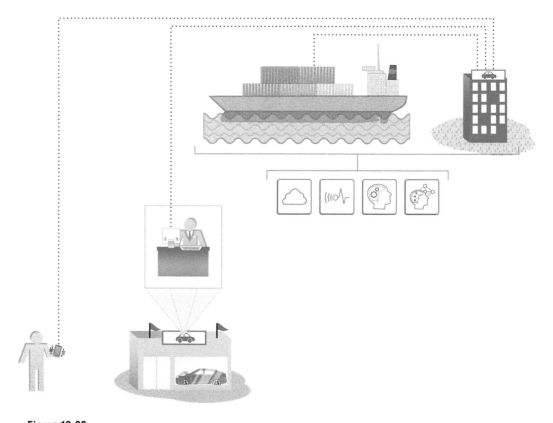

Figure 12.23

The customer and the sales person can view the location of the car as it is being transported to the dealership. Because the device is attached to the car itself, its location can be tracked, whether it is being delivered via a cargo boat, a truck or both. The primary back-end technologies that enable this feature are cloud computing and IoT. Machine learning and AI technologies are also involved in the data processing.

The tracking information is made available via a mobile app and a web app. Customers use the mobile app, which queries the tracking data and displays the location of the car on a map whenever the app is opened. The web app is typically used by the sales person to view the location of the car from a workstation (Figure 12.24).

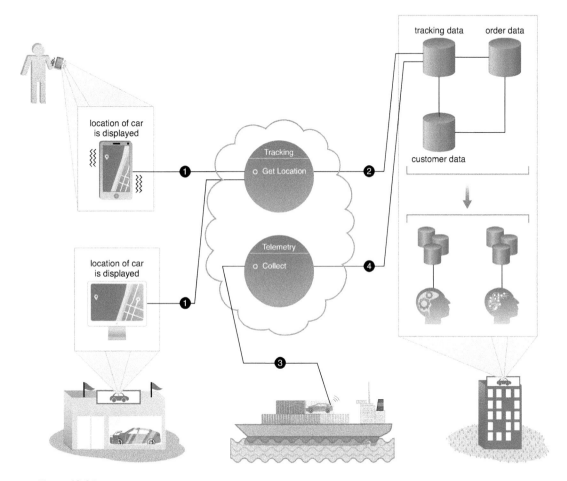

Figure 12.24

When the customer or sales person opens the app, it invokes the Tracking service to request the car's current location (1). The Tracking service interacts with the organization's IT back end to return the most current tracking information (2). The IoT device on the car carries out telemetry data capture by transmitting its GPS coordinates back to the car manufacturer's office on a frequent and regular basis via the Telemetry service (3, 4), which is part of a greater IoT system. Using data streaming, the tracking data is transmitted to and recorded on the back end, and the geographic location is periodically updated in the car's order record. The frequency at which the customer checks the location is further recorded as part of the customer data in the customer profile. Both the collected operations (tracking, order) data and customer data are made available to machine learning and AI systems for future model training, analysis and reporting, and automated decision-making purposes.

> **NOTE**
>
> This step provides somewhat of an omni-channel experience, in that there is omni-channel support for the customer to obtain the location of the car. The customer can use the mobile app, call the sales person or visit the car dealership in person and each inquiry can be logged as part of the customer data in the customer profile. However, it is not a prime example of omni-channel support as the customer is not actually furthering the overall task of purchasing the car by inquiring about its transit location. Furthermore, the customer is expected to rely primarily on the use of the mobile app.

Step 13. Dealership Provides Car

When the car arrives at the dealership, the GPS device is removed and the car is professionally cleaned, washed and waxed. The dealership further gives the customer some complimentary items (such as a keychain holder and a hat with the car's logo) as a means of thanking the customer via rewardful warmth. The customer then takes ownership of the car (Figure 12.25).

Figure 12.25
Upon the customer arriving, the sales person presents the freshly cleaned car to the customer, along with the keys and some gifts.

Step 14. Dealership Offers Plan

Before the customer leaves with the car, the sales person offers the customer a complimentary car monitoring and road-side assistance plan. This is an attempt at providing an extent of rewardful warmth by supplying the customer's car with monitoring and road-side assistance at no charge for one year (Figure 12.26). The sales person explains that a device will be installed in the car to transmit usage and location information back to the dealership and the car manufacturer's office on a regular basis.

The intent is to carry out a relationship-value action that will help the dealership stay on top of the car's maintenance requirements. It will also help the car manufacturer predetermine potential wear issues with the car before they become a problem. In exchange for consent from the customer to share customer data (such as car usage and location data) with the car manufacturer, the plan will provide roadside assistance services at no charge, so that if the car ever breaks down or the customer needs help, a service vehicle will be dispatched to aid the customer.

Figure 12.26

The sales person offers a complimentary car monitoring and road-side assistance plan to the customer. This involves the use of cloud computing technology on the back end.

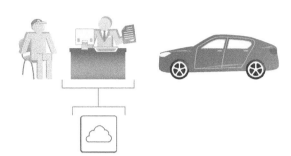

When the sales person requests the plan online it is provided with all of the customer data and car information pre-filled (Figure 12.27).

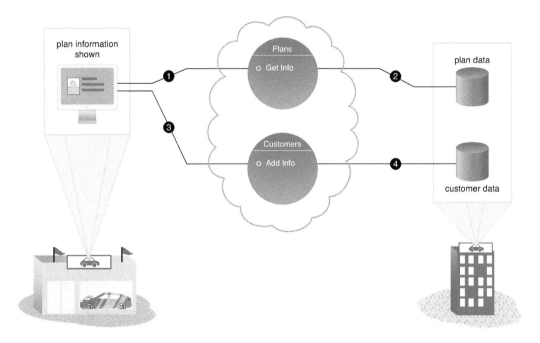

Figure 12.27

The sales person uses the workstation to request the latest version of the plan via the Plans service (1). The fact that the plan was offered to the customer is further recorded as part of the customer data in the customer's profile via the Customers service (2).

Step 15. Customer Accepts Plan?

If the customer decides not to order the plan, proceed to Step 16.

If the customer does order the plan, proceed to Step 17.

Step 16. Customer Takes Unmonitored Car

The customer decides not to proceed with the complimentary monitoring and road-side assistance plan, and consequently leaves the dealership with the unmonitored car (Figure 12.28).

Figure 12.28
The customer journey ends with the customer taking the new car and leaving the dealership. The attempt at carrying out a relationship-value action via rewardful warmth failed, which is recorded on the back end. This step involves cloud computing, machine learning and AI technologies.

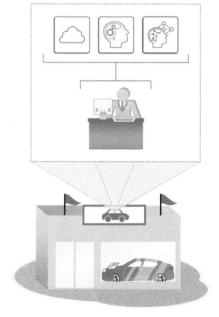

Upon confirming that the customer is not proceeding with the second product (the plan), the sales person updates the customer profile with a "rejected" status associated with the proposed plan, which is then further recorded as part of both customer data and operations data in the digital transformation solution (Figure 12.29).

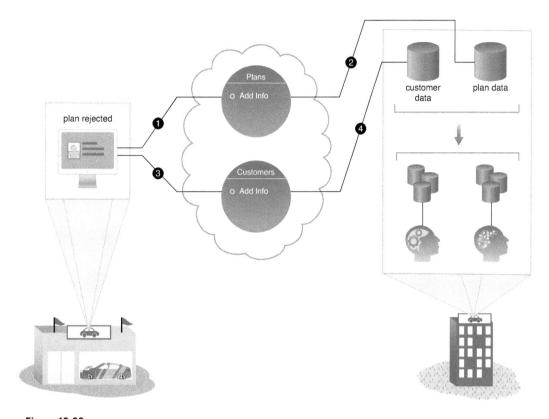

Figure 12.29

The fact that the plan was rejected by the customer is recorded as part of the plan data and customer data via the use of the Plans (1, 2) and Customers (3, 4) services, respectively. This new data is made available to machine learning and AI systems as new input that these systems can use for future model training, analysis and reporting, and automated decision-making purposes.

Step 17. Process Order and Update Account

The customer decides to proceed with the complimentary monitoring and road-side assistance plan. As part of completing the paperwork for the plan, the sales person is required to ask the customer about what types of activity the customer is willing to share usage information about via the built-in sensor.

If the customer has data privacy concerns, the amount of data being monitored and shared will be limited. However, the sales person points out that limiting the data may also limit the extent to which the car manufacturer can proactively assist the customer in avoiding and addressing potential car maintenance issues.

Once the customer indicates the extent to which data can be shared, the sales person places the order for the plan (Figure 12.30). The sales person receives an immediate reply confirming that the plan is approved and active.

Figure 12.30

The customer proceeds with the plan, which is then ordered and considered a transaction that is part of a relationship-value action. The technologies involved in this step are cloud computing, blockchain, machine learning and AI.

The monitoring and road-side assistance plan is not customized for each customer. Instead, a vanilla plan agreement is submitted and processed as an order. For auditing purposes, this is considered a legal transaction. The fact that the customer's car will be monitored under this plan is further recorded in the back-end customer data (Figure 12.31).

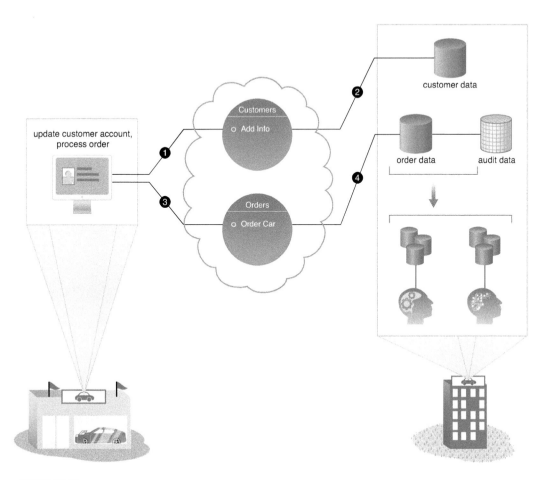

Figure 12.31

The sales person's workstation submits the order for the plan via the Orders service (1), which interacts with the organization's IT back end to register the order and store select order data in the immutable blockchain audit data repository (2) for historical record keeping purposes. The acceptance of the plan is then further registered in the customer profile via the Customers service (3, 4). The newly updated customer data and operations data are made available to machine learning and AI systems as new input that these systems can use for future model training, analysis and reporting, and automated decision-making purposes.

Step 18. Sensor Installed in Car

The customer waits while a mechanic installs the monitoring sensor in the customer's car (Figure 12.32). The sensor is then linked with the car manufacturer's back end so that an on-going connection is maintained from thereon. This relationship-value action is expected to extend the existing customer journey (and introduce new customer journeys) by extending the duration of the relationship with the customer.

Figure 12.32
The mechanic installs an IoT device with a sensor that connects with a greater IoT system via the cloud.

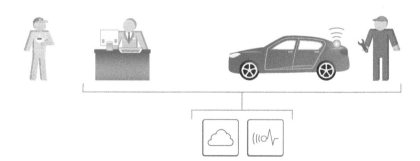

Once the device is installed and activated, the sales person links the customer's account with the tracking system. Telemetry data capture is then used to record the customer's tracking history that is then stored as part of the operations (tracking) data and the historical customer data (Figure 12.33).

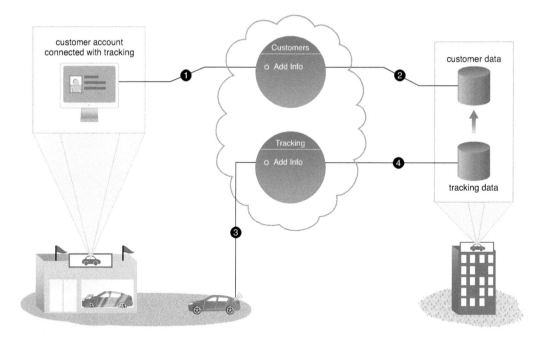

Figure 12.33
The sales person's workstation updates the customer profile account via the Customers service (1, 2), which links it to the monitoring system in the organization's IT back end. The IoT sensor on the car establishes a link via the Tracking service (3) and the greater IoT system so that future transit by and usage of the car is tracked, stored and linked to the customer data in the customer profile (4).

Step 19. Customer Takes Monitored Car

The customer leaves with the new car, which is now monitored via the installed device (Figure 12.34).

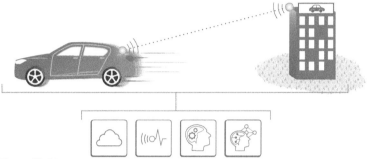

Figure 12.34

The monitored car will remain linked with and monitored by the car manufacturer. The technologies involved in this on-going flow of data include cloud computing, IoT, machine learning and AI.

The customer's car remains connected with the car manufacturer via the sensor on the installed IoT device. The data associated with the car's future transit activity, motor functions and the usage of some of its other features will be collected and stored with the car manufacturer (Figure 12.35).

NOTE
With the customer's consent, the collected telemetry data could also be shared with third-party organizations. For example, the data could be provided to an insurance company that may choose to adjust the customer's insurance rate based on the monitored driving habits.

Step 20. Dealership Follows Up

After a period of time, the sales person follows up to remind the customer that a maintenance check should be scheduled and/or that a part of the car requires attention (Figure 12.36). In response to this proactive warmth by the dealership, the customer subsequently visits the dealership to have the car serviced.

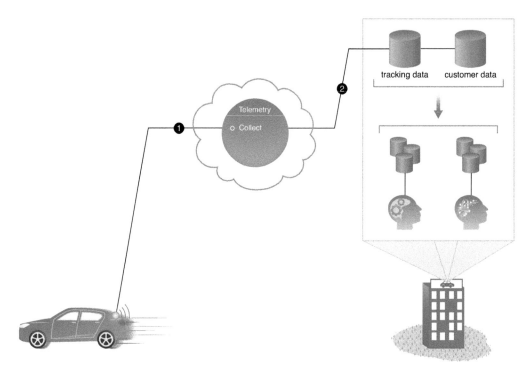

Figure 12.35

While the car is in use or in transit, the installed IoT device makes a periodic connection with the Telemetry service (1) to off-load any collected activity data. The Telemetry service, as part of a greater IoT system, transmits the tracking data to the organization's IT back end where it is stored and linked to the customer profile (2). The updated customer data and operations data are made available to machine learning and AI systems as new input that these systems can use for future model training, analysis and reporting, and automated decision-making purposes.

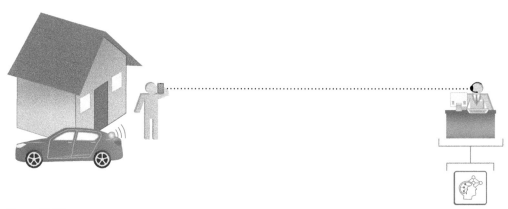

Figure 12.36

The customer is contacted by the sales person who suggests that the car be brought in for a service visit. This communication is initiated by a request by the back-end AI system.

The AI system responsible for processing the tracking data receives sufficient event data and alerts via telemetry data capture to determine that the car should be scheduled for a service visit. The AI system consequently notifies the sales person to contact the customer (Figure 12.37) to request a visit via communicative warmth.

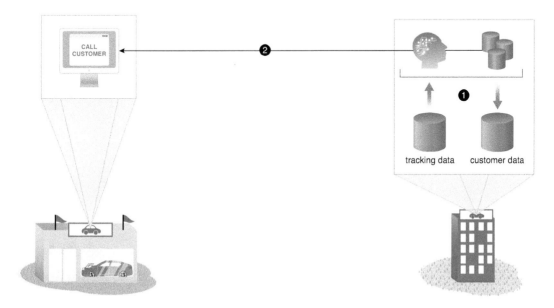

Figure 12.37
Tracking data is processed by the AI system that eventually carries out intelligent automated decision-making to determine that the customer should be contacted. The customer data is correspondingly updated (1) and a notification is sent to the sales person's workstation (2) to reach out to the customer.

Step 21. Dealership Offers Trade-in

After a longer period of time, the sales person notifies the customer of an opportunity to trade-in the customer's current car for a new model with new features and improvements (Figure 12.38).

The AI system in the car manufacturer's IT back end has been continually processing the following customer data and operations data relevant to this stage in the customer journey:

- The transit tracking data for the customer's car, as the car's mileage continued to increase and it was subjected to more wear.

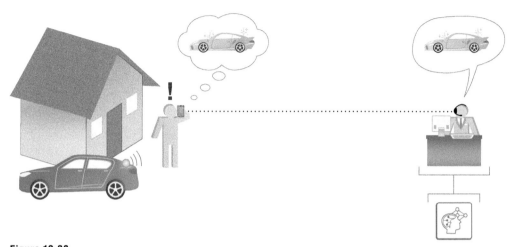

Figure 12.38

The customer has owned the car for a while and it is no longer new. The sales person, in another act of proactive warmth, approaches the customer about trading it in for a newer model.

- The utilization tracking data that provided insights as to how the customer used the car, where it was driven to, what features of the car were used most frequently and perhaps even how often passengers were inside (and for how long).

- The current car product data that the AI system attempts to match with what it knows of the customer's preferences, driving habits and other aspects of the customer as recorded in the customer profile that has been developed and refined over time.

Many other types of input data might be included in this analysis. When the AI system reaches a point where it determines it has sufficient data and the timing is right, it decides that the customer should be contacted regarding a trade-in.

As part of this outreach, the back end generates an online car design with features and add-ons tailored to the customer's known preferences and adds the car design to the customer's profile on the mobile app (Figure 12.39).

> **NOTE**
>
> The digital transformation solution's omni-channel support will enable the customer to explore further customizations to the new car design remotely, via the mobile app, that the dealership will already be aware of if the customer should return.

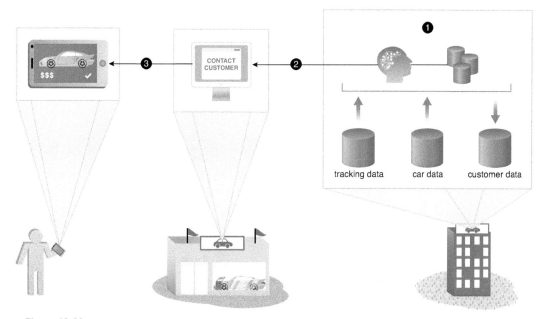

Figure 12.39

The AI system has been processing and analyzing data regarding the customer and the associated car usage for a long time (1). It reaches a point where it carries out intelligent automated decision-making to determine that the customer is likely ready to trade in the previously purchased car for a specific new model (2). The sales person is provided with an online design for the new proposed car model and is instructed to forward that car design to the customer's mobile app (3) and then follow up with a phone call to further explain the trade-in opportunity via communicative warmth.

Step 1: Customer Visits Dealership (Again)

If the customer agrees to consider trading in the older car for a new model, the customer returns to the dealership to start the journey over again (Figure 12.40). This time, the business process may not only be focused on the purchase of the next new car, but also on the fostering of the long-term customer relationship itself.

The fact that the customer has demonstrated loyalty by returning to the dealership after all this time increases the customer's value to the company. Additional steps may therefore be incorporated to further reward customer loyalty in support of this customer (trading in and) purchasing more new cars in the future.

Figure 12.40

The customer returns to the dealership to inquire about the new car model. When successfully building and maintaining long-term relationships with customers, this type of return business cycle can iterate indefinitely.

Come back soon!

I will!

Our ultimate goal is to establish mutually beneficial, long-term relationships with our customers, as this leads to business stability and on-going opportunities for business growth.

Future Decision-Making

With each customer that completes the car purchasing business process, new data is collected and processed. This is further supplemented with the repeated data ingress of new third-party data. Over time, this on-going accumulation of new data can increase both the quantity and quality of the data intelligence made available to the car manufacturer.

This leads to two primary business opportunities:

- Use new and refined data intelligence to improve existing lines of business.

- Use new and refined data intelligence to discover insights that lead to new innovations and new lines of business.

In other words, the underlying data science technologies are not only used in support of digital transformation solutions and to improve individual customer journeys; they are also used to deliver data intelligence to decision makers within the car manufacturing organization to support them in determining the strategic direction of the company itself (Figure 12.41).

Figure 12.41

A decision maker at the car manufacturing company uses the latest available data intelligence to carry out intelligent manual decision-making that will impact the strategic direction of the business.

About the Authors

Thomas Erl

Thomas Erl is a best-selling IT author who has authored and co-authored 15 books published by Prentice Hall and Pearson Education and dedicated to topics focused on contemporary information technology and practices. These titles were delivered for the *Pearson Digital Enterprise Series from Thomas Erl* (formerly the *Prentice Hall Service Technology Series from Thomas Erl*) for which Thomas also acts as series editor.

As founder and president of Arcitura Education (www.arcitura.com), Thomas also leads the development of curricula for internationally recognized, vendor-neutral training and accreditation programs. Arcitura's portfolio currently consists of over 100 courses, over 90 Pearson VUE exams and over 40 certification tracks, covering topics such as Digital Transformation, Robotic Process Automation (RPA), DevOps, Blockchain, IoT, Containerization, Machine Learning, Artificial Intelligence (AI), Cybersecurity, Service-Oriented Architecture (SOA), Cloud Computing and Big Data Analytics.

Roger Stoffers

Roger is a TOGAF-certified Enterprise Architect passionate about Digital Transformation and Integration. Roger has worked for (and with) organizations in Telecommunication, Government and Finance industries, building 25 years of experience in multinational organizations. He has served as principal and lead Enterprise Domain Architect for digital business transformation initiatives, with strong focus for customer relationships and sustainable organizational agility in distributed environments.

Presently Roger works as Enterprise Architect for de Volksbank, fostering Customer Centricity and the organization's Sustainability & Social Responsibility goals with Data-Driven Customer Engagement and Decisioning.

Independently, Roger is a worldwide consulting architect for digital transformation and integration, and a senior trainer for (enterprise) architecture topics and contemporary vendor-neutral technology and next-generation IT topics. He is a speaker at conferences about Digital Transformation, SOA and Microservices and Enterprise Architecture.

He is a contributor for the Service-Oriented Architecture: Analysis and Design for Services and Microservices book from the Pearson Digital Enterprise Series from Thomas Erl.

Index

ABOUT THE SERIES

The Pearson Digital Enterprise Series from Thomas Erl aims to provide the IT industry with comprehensive, unbiased coverage of the contemporary practices and technology innovations that are driving the international adoption and evolution of digital transformation and the realization of digital enterprises. Each title in this book series is authored in relation to other titles so as to establish a library of complementary knowledge. Although the series covers a broad spectrum of topics, each title is authored in compliance with common language, vocabulary, and illustration conventions so as to enable readers to continually explore cross-topic research and education.

 DigitalEnterpriseBookSeries.com

ABOUT THE SERIES EDITOR

Thomas Erl is a best-selling IT author and the series editor of the Pearson Digital Enterprise Series from Thomas Erl. As CEO of Arcitura Education Inc., Thomas has led the development of curricula for the internationally recognized Digital Transformation Professional Academy and the Next-Gen IT Academy, as well as the Big Data Science Certified Professional (BDSCP), Cloud Certified Professional (CCP), and SOA Certified Professional (SOACP) accreditation programs. These programs have established a series of formal, vendor-neutral industry certifications with over 100 courses, over 90 Pearson VUE exams, and over 40 certification tracks.

Thomas has toured more than 20 countries as a speaker and instructor. He has over 100 articles and interviews published in numerous publications, including the Wall Street Journal and CIO Magazine. Several of his books have become international bestsellers and have been formally endorsed by senior members of major IT organizations, such as IBM, Microsoft, Oracle, Intel, Accenture, IEEE, HL7, MITRE, SAP, CISCO, HP, and many others.

A Field Guide to Digital Transformation
by T. Erl, R. Stoffers

ISBN: 9780137571840
Paperback, 278 pages

Service-Oriented Architecture: Analysis & Design for Services and Microservices (Second Edition)
by T. Erl, P. Merson, R. Stoffers

ISBN: 9780133858587
Paperback, 393 pages

Big Data Fundamentals: Concepts, Drivers & Techniques
by P. Buhler, T. Erl, W. Khattaks

ISBN: 9780134291079
Paperback, 218 pages

Cloud Computing Design Patterns
by T. Erl, R. Cope, A. Naserpour

ISBN: 9780133858563
Paperback, 564 pages

Next Generation SOA: A Concise Introduction to Service Technology & Service-Orientation
by T. Erl, C. Gee, J. Kress, B. Maier, H. Normann, P. Raj, L Shuster, B. Trops, C. Utschig-Utschig, P. Wik, T. Winterberg

ISBN: 9780133859041
Paperback, 208 pages

SOA with Java: Realizing Service-Orientation with Java Technologies
by T. Erl, S. Roy, P. Thomas, A. Tost

ISBN: 9780133859034
Paperback, 590 pages

Cloud Computing: Concepts, Technology & Architecture
by T. Erl, Z. Mahmood, R. Puttini

ISBN: 9780133387520
Paperback, 528 pages

SOA with REST: Principles, Patterns & Constraints for Building Enterprise Solutions with REST
by R. Balasubramanian, B. Carlyle, T. Erl, C. Pautasso

ISBN: 9780137012510
Paperback, 577 pages

SOA Governance: Governing Shared Services On-Premise & in the Cloud
by S. Bennett, T. Erl, C. Gee, R. Laird, A. Manes, R. Schneider, L. Shuster, A. Tost, C. Venable

ISBN: 9780138156756
Paperback, 675 pages

SOA with .NET & Windows Azure: Realizing Service-Orientation with the Microsoft Platform
by D. Chou, J. de Vadoss, T. Erl, N. Gandhi, H. Kommalapati, B. Loesgen, C. Schittko, H. Wilhelmsen, M. Williams

ISBN: 9780131582316
Paperback, 893 pages

SOA Design Patterns
by T. Erl

ISBN: 9780136135166
Paperback, 865 pages

Web Service Contract Design and Versioning for SOA
by T. Erl, H. Haas, A. Karmarkar, C. Liu, D. Orchard, J. Pasley, A. Tost, P. Walmsley, U. Yalcinalp

ISBN: 9780136135173
Paperback, 826 pages

SOA Principles of Service Design
by T. Erl

ISBN: 9780132344821
Paperback, 573 pages

Service-Oriented Architecture: Concepts, Technology, and Design
by T. Erl

ISBN: 9780131858589
Paperback, 760 pages

Service-Oriented Architecture: A Field Guide to Integrating XML and Web Services
by T. Erl

ISBN: 9780131428980
Paperback, 534 pages

Digital Transformation Certification Tracks
DIGITAL TRANSFORMATION PROFESSIONAL ACADEMY

		Digital Transformation Specialist	Digital Transformation Technology Professional	Digital Transformation Technology Architect	Digital Transformation Data Science Professional	Digital Transformation Data Scientist	Digital Transformation Security Professional	Digital Transformation Security Specialist	Digital Transformation IA Professional	Digital Transformation IA Specialist
MODULE 01	Fundamental Digital Transformation	●	●	●	●	●	●	●	●	●
MODULE 02	Digital Transformation in Practice	●	●	●	●	●	●	●	●	●
MODULE 03	Fundamental Cloud Computing		●	●						
MODULE 04	Fundamental Blockchain		●	●		●	●			
MODULE 05	Fundamental IoT		●	●						
MODULE 06	Cloud Architecture			●						
MODULE 07	Blockchain Architecture			●				●		
MODULE 08	IoT Architecture			●						
MODULE 09	Fundamental Big Data Analysis & Analytics				●	●				
MODULE 10	Fundamental Machine Learning				●	●				
MODULE 11	Fundamental AI				●	●			●	●
MODULE 12	Advanced Big Data Analysis & Analytics					●				
MODULE 13	Advanced Machine Learning					●				
MODULE 14	Advanced AI					●				●
MODULE 15	Fundamental Cybersecurity						●	●		
MODULE 16	Advanced Cybersecurity							●		
MODULE 17	Fundamental RPA								●	●
MODULE 18	Advanced RPA									●